A Bottle of Notes
and Some Voyages

Germano Celant

**A Bottle of Notes
and Some Voyages**

**Claes Oldenburg
Coosje van Bruggen**

Claes Oldenburg:

Drawings, Sculptures,
and Large-Scale Projects
with Coosje van Bruggen

Published by Northern Centre
for Contemporary Art, Sunderland
and The Henry Moore Centre
for the Study of Sculpture
Leeds City Art Galleries
1988

Distributed in Great Britain
and Northern Ireland
and at the European exhibition venues
by Northern Centre for Contemporary Art
17 Grange Terrace, Stockton Road
Sunderland SR2 7DF
ISBN 0 904461 94 7

Distributed in other countries
by Rizzoli International Publications, Inc
597 Fifth Avenue, New York, NY 10017
ISBN 0 8478 0946 3
LC 87 63414

Graphic Design
Pierluigi Cerri

Assistant
Sue O'Brien

Printed in England by
W. S. Maney and Son Ltd, Leeds

A Bottle of Notes
and Some Voyages

Sponsored by
The Henry Moore Foundation
MoMart Ltd, London
Leeds City Council
The Museums and Galleries Commission
Northern Arts
Sunderland Borough Council
Visiting Arts

Northern Centre for Contemporary Art
Sunderland
2 February–26 March 1988

The Henry Moore Centre
for the Study of Sculpture
Leeds City Art Gallery
27 April–26 June 1988

The Serpentine Gallery, London
9 July–29 August 1988

The Glynn Vivian Art Gallery
and Museum, Swansea
17 September–12 November 1988

Note: Unless otherwise stated
exhibits are from the collection
of the artist.
Captions for illustrations:
height precedes width.

Tony Knipe, Director
Northern Centre for Contemporary Art
Sunderland

Dr Terry Friedman, Principal Keeper
The Henry Moore Centre
for the Study of Sculpture
Leeds City Art Galleries

Foreword

No other major sculptor of our time has revealed the hidden potencies of everyday objects with such penetrating aptness, quick-wittedness and daring as Claes Oldenburg. He has seen in *Giant Ice-Bag* the dome of the United States Capitol, and contrived a huge *Lipstick Ascending on Caterpillar Tracks* as a platform for student speeches (the speaker mounting the tracks and pumping up the stick to get attention, the stick sinking down after the speech), and a *Cemetery in the Shape of a Colossal Screw Skyscraper*, intended for São Paolo, which, as it is filled with coffins, screws into the earth until only the head projects above ground as a memorial. The associations are remarkable because the artist makes crucial leaps from everyday objects to extraordinary images by-passing the obvious.

It has been a matter of regret, therefore, that the work of this internationally acclaimed sculptor has not been seen to any significant extent in Britain for seventeen years, since the occasion of the Tate Gallery retrospective in 1970, for there are otherwise few examples of his work in public collections in this country, with the result that an entire generation is likely to know his art only second-hand. The present exhibition sets out to redress this imbalance. It is hoped that it will serve not only as a source of wonder and delight, but as a demonstration of the brilliant and audacious achievement of a great artist.

The exhibition is a retrospective of work from the 1960s to the present and covers a wide range of Claes Oldenburg's preoccupations; these have been influenced by the ideas of Coosje van Bruggen, the artist's wife, and she has collaborated in all the large-scale projects since 1976. They are represented by sketchbook drawings and models, among which are such legendary Oldenburgian images as the cocktail, the drum set, the fireplug, the flashlight and the Geometric Mouse. Eight projects form the show's nucleus: *Three-way Plug*, *Screwarch*, *Toothbrush*, *Blasted Pencil*, *Matchcover*, *The Haunted House*, *Piano Hammock* and *Bottle of Notes*. Of these, the twenty-two foot long *Extinguished Match*, the group of sculptures making up *The Haunted House*, and *Piano Hammock*, all projects dating from 1987,

appear in their final, heroic size. Clearly the monumental scale of others, such as *Giant Trowel* at Otterlo, *Batcolumn* in Chicago or *Flashlight* at Las Vegas, ranging from 12 to 33 metres high and fastened to their sites, could not be accommodated in an exhibition intended to tour in Britain and on the Continent. *Three-way Plug* and *Cross-section of a Toothbrush with Paste, in a Cup, on a Sink: Portrait of Coosje's Thinking* are represented by large working models, and these as well as the other large-scale projects in the show are accompanied by smaller models, drawings and prints. *Match Cover*, for Barcelona, and *Bottle of Notes*, on the theme of Captain Cook and proposed for Middlesbrough, are works-in-progress.

This variety offers unusual insights into the sculptor's working methods, from ideas through sketches, small and large models to finished sculptures, and reveals how stereotypical objects, the substance of Claes Oldenburg's repertory, are startlingly transformed through radical changes of scale, materials and environments into new objects which remain familiar in appearance but no longer possess their original meaning or function. Thus, Disney's Mickey Mouse is transformed into a lollipop, a kite, a blimp and a balloon with a hot-dog nose; a melting butter pat and a slice of blueberry pie are the structures of prospective summerhouses; a grand piano is made to resemble Alcatraz (in another project the island is replaced by a baked potato with butter), or, ship-wrecked on a Cuban beach, becomes an image signifying 'the wreck of the Old World stranded on the shore of the New'; in turn, the piano lid is refashioned into an office building proposed for Venice, Italy.

Though a comic strain runs through much of Claes Oldenburg's work, he and Coosje van Bruggen also confront deeply serious issues, as is revealed particularly in *The Blasted Pencil (Which Still Writes)*, as yet an unrealised large-scale project for the University of El Salvador, which during the last few decades has been plagued by a tragic succession of repressive regimes, and which are movingly chronicled in an essay written by Ms van Bruggen.

The exhibits were selected by Claes Oldenburg and Coosje van Bruggen; to both we are

profoundly grateful. That the idea of this exhibition originated as a collaboration between two institutions based in the North of England, Northern Centre for Contemporary Art at Sunderland, Tyne and Wear, and The Henry Moore Centre for the Study of Sculpture at Leeds City Art Galleries, Yorkshire, should come as no surprise. Both Sunderland and Leeds have championed the causes of modern art over many years, and they have long been interested in Claes Oldenburg's work: the former having included a group of sketches in *Drawing in Air: An exhibition of sculptor's drawings 1882–1982*, 1983 (which toured to Leeds), the latter having acquired work by the artist, including the 1966 drawing *Fagends in the Park*, from an unrealised Kensington Gardens project, and *Miniature Soft Drum Set* of 1969. Moreover, Northern Centre has been closely involved with *Bottle of Notes* for Middlesbrough, the first large-scale project by the sculptor likely to be realised in Britain.

The exhibition and its publication have received generous support from a number of sources, listed separately, among which the organisers express their particular thanks to The Henry Moore Foundation and MoMart Ltd, London. The Beijer Collection and Moderna Museet, Stockholm, William J. Hokin (Century America Corporation), the Krannert Art Museum, University of Illinois, Leo Castelli Gallery, New York, Gilbert and Lila Silverman and the artist have generously lent works. Germano Celant, Gerhard Storck, Claes Oldenburg and Coosje van Bruggen have contributed important essays to the publication, which has been designed by Pierluigi Cerri and Sue O'Brien of Gregotti Associati, Milan, and printed by W.S. Maney and Son Ltd, Leeds, under the watchful eye of Peter McGrath. The assistance of Marja-Liisa Bell, Scott Blyth, Kaatje Cusse, Bryan Dovey, Jennifer Hallam, Claus Henning, Terry McCartney, Henry Meric Hughes, Jim Moyes, Sue Priestley, Stephanie Teychenne, Alister Warman, Heather Wilson and the Museums and Galleries Commission has immeasurably enriched this enterprise. We also thank Dr Cristoph Brockhaus, Peter Davies, Roger Hall, Les Hooper, Knud Jensen, Dr Gottlieb Leinz, Leeds Photo Litho and Stephen McNulty.

Contents

6/8/83

spider

170-83

Introduction and Essay

Facing page:
*Notebook Page: Basketball in Net,
on a Cliff Overlooking the Pacific Ocean*
1983
Pencil, felt pen
Two sheets 5 × 2¾ in (12.7 × 7 cm)
on sheet 11 × 8½ in (28 × 21 cm)

Aboard the Broome Street

Claes Oldenburg

After fifteen years on the Lower East Side of Manhattan, I moved in 1971 to the West side of the island, taking over the Marine Engine Specialities Corporation on Broome Street. When I first saw the company's two adjoining five-storey buildings, they were filled with wooden models of propellers and other ship parts. These were soon replaced by all my work and archives.

Coosje's and my first task, on moving into the buildings in 1978, was to inventory the accumulated material and select what was worth keeping. Old works were placed in new situations, such as the parts of the sculpture called *A Broken Plate of Scrambled Eggs* from 1965, which were rescued by Coosje out of a pile of debris, and hung on our dining room wall, where they eventually contributed to the *Dropped Bowl with Scattered Slices and Peels*, our fountain for Miami.

In the mornings while I slept, Coosje roamed the upper floors of the buildings, taking snapshots of found objects and objects in process. One consequence of the inventory was the final and definitive version of the collection known as the *Mouse Museum*, to which was added the *Ray Gun Wing*, containing accumulated objects in the shape of guns. Besides a lot of found cultural bric-a-brac which had served as inspiration, many small studies for sculptures were placed into these museums. Afterwards Coosje wrote a history of my work based on the objects in the collection.

Our collaboration began in the Netherlands, with the reconstruction and relocation of the *Giant Trowel* in 1976, at the Rijksmuseum Kröller-Müller in Otterlo, and proceeded through the installation of the *Giant Pool Balls* in Münster, West Germany, in 1977, done during the year and a half that we lived in Deventer, a town 100 km east of Amsterdam. After that, we moved to Broome Street and began concentrating our activity in the direction of 'feasible monuments' or 'large-scale projects', as Coosje later renamed them.

Our commissions start with a visit to the site to gather information, which is brought back to be mixed with the contents of Broome Street. When the mixture, after several months, yields an emblem combining our identity with that of the site, I proceed to make a presentation model, often rapidly, by improvising with materials at hand.

Coosje described the nature and limits of Broome Street execution in 1978: 'With the passage of time the contents of the studio grow in an organic way into a kind of city landscape that reflects the world outside the studio through the accumulation of material such as ripped-out advertisements, maps, and small purchased and found objects. Besides this there are fragments of thoughts hastily typed or scribbled, sketches, 'studio objects', remnants of work processes, and an abundance of 'living' material: pieces of rope, metal and plastic wire, plaster, muslin, glue, styrofoam, foam rubber, canvas, kapok, staples etc. etc. Techniques used in the studio are purposely kept on the primitive level of a Robinson Crusoe. A broken compass has to be taped together before it can be used. Two strings serve as an aid in rendering perspective.'[1] Though at this stage the important thing is the idea and the model may be rough and abbreviated, it must give a convincing impression of the end result. There is usually a 'figure for scale', made of a nail driven into the base, wrapped with tape and painted black, for the observer to identify with.

Besides our collaboration, Coosje is a writer on art and a free-lance curator, with her own area of Broome Street, secluded and orderly, quite

Broome Street, New York City
1976. The Studio consists of two
interconnecting buildings.

The association of Broome Street with a ship
was encouraged by the previous tenants who
inscribed 'Ahead' and 'Astern' on the
controls of the room-size elevator which
moves at a leisurely pace between the floors.
It is an association felt strongly in the late
afternoons when the inhabitants are as sealed
off from the surroundings as on a ship at sea,
because of the thousands of honking cars and
trucks trying to force their way into the
nearby Holland Tunnel, our link to mainland
America. And also during nights of high
wind, when the plain maple boards of the
floors, laid like decks over raw wooden
beams, creak like a rolling hull.

different from the rest. In working with me, she accepts my approach of using objects and transforming them, but brings to it her distinct personality and ideas, political, social and aesthetic. Though Coosje does not hand-make any of the models or drawings, she often defines the position or treatment of a subject.

Deciding that the *Spoonbridge* needed a 'contrapposto', she reached into the shelves at Broome Street for a wooden cherry with a gesturing nail-stem (from the top of a sundae made of little coloured bags of sand) and placed it on the spoon I had brought up from the kitchen to bend and glue on a model of the site.

Coosje turned the *Flashlight* model around, making a faint glow against the ground, to contrast it with the spectacular use of light in Las Vegas. After proposing the *Button* for the campus of the University of Pennsylvania, she split the model to create 'the most discarded object' she could imagine, which might have fallen off a harried student's shirt. She tilted the model of the *Spitzhacke* slightly to the side, because she felt that the object would become more interesting if it showed the touch of a human being. In choice of subject, or in any detail, in form or colour, there is no part of a large-scale project Coosje cannot determine, with my hand responsive to her words.

Each project is a journey, which may last as long as two or three years, at the end of which we gather the documents into a case history.

One evening in 1983, while discussing a commission for a site in La Jolla at the University of California, San Diego, which was near the Scripps Institution of Oceanography, we noted the difference between the Institution's approach to sea life, which is to catch a fish and let it go, with that of the project's backer, a commercial tuna fisherman operating in the same seas. The following morning, Coosje woke up with a motto on her lips: 'Caught and set free!' Looking for some distance from the subject, we decided to substitute a basketball net and ball. The site was by an Indian burial ground; this evoked a feathered head-dress which contributed to a drawing of the proposal. Because the site was on a cliff overlooking the Pacific Ocean, the ball sliding through the net was equated with the sun slipping over the Western horizon. The basketball could separate slightly at the seams, to let in light: the ball thus became a room. It would be entered through the hoop, approached through a kind of garden space surrounded by a giant net. The motto 'Caught and Set Free!' could be inscribed somewhere inside, in the centre or on the spherical walls. Later we heard that the University was opposed to being identified with basketball; besides that, the cliff site near the laboratory became unavailable, which caused us to lose interest.

At about the same time, we were considering another site, in Gore Creek, a stream that runs through the resort town of Vail, Colorado, in the Rocky Mountains. We felt that a fishing pole would be good there, as it had an affinity with old-time bamboo ski-poles and the tension lines of the gondola that carries the skiers up to the slopes. The most critical part of the sculpture was what would be at the end of the line. We were thinking of fishlines in comic-strips, which always bring up an interesting object. Coosje proposed a rusty tin can, which seemed especially appropriate, as the metallic debris of many a Rockies' prospector lies buried in the bed of the stream. For Coosje the can also became a statement about 'the clutter caused by human beings.' At a hearing in defence of the proposal, I was able to produce a catalogue of similar debris obtained from the stream-bed. For my part I saw great sculptural possibilities in the transformation of a rusty tin can with a ragged bent-up lid, engaged on a huge, shiny fishing hook, and made a rather elaborate presentation model. Though the sculpture was approved, it became tied up in a property dispute. After a while we withdrew, convinced that the real obstacle was the rusty tin can, when what they wanted was a leaping trout. In any case, the *Arch in the Form of Fishing Pole with a Line and Can* also remains an unsited work.

So far we have managed to bring eighteen works to completion. Several have gotten away from us, perhaps because we strayed too far from the reality principle; but we would rather risk rejection than put restraints on our imaginations. The large-scale projects are, after all, the descendants of the Proposed Colossal Monuments of the Sixties.

Preliminary Model for an Arch in the Form of a Fishing Pole, a Line and Can for Vail, Colorado
1983
Cardboard, wood, steel; painted
3 parts
2 parts each 22½ × 15 in (57.2 × 38.1 cm)
1 part 50 × 15 in (127 × 38.1 cm)
Height 36 in (91.4 cm)
Collection Charles Rosenquist
Vail, Colorado

[1] Coosje van Bruggen, *Claes Oldenburg: Mouse Museum/Ray Gun Wing*, 1979

Proposal for a Building in the Form of a
Colossal Flashlight in Place of the Hoover
Dam, Nevada
1982
Crayon on paper
40 × 30 in (102 × 76 cm)

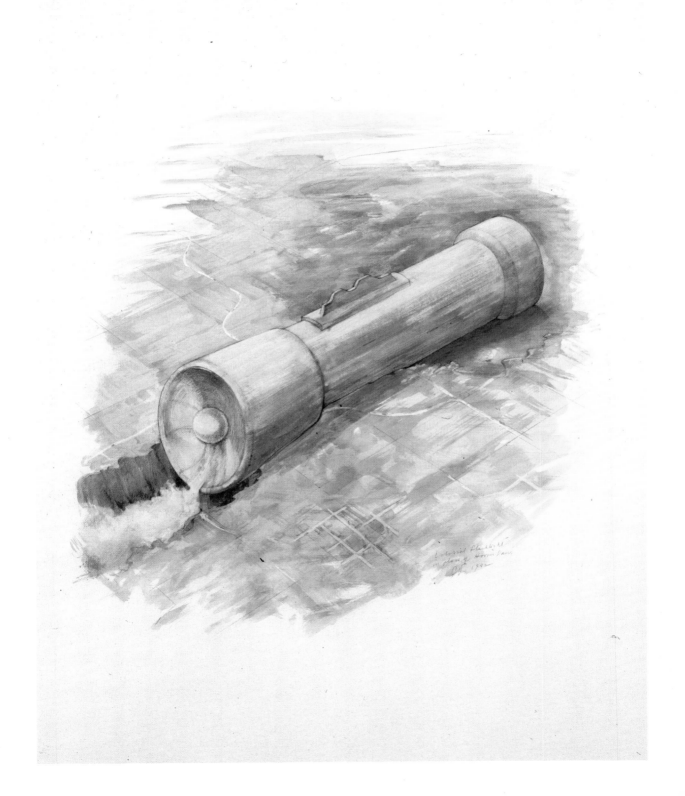

In and Out of the Bottle

Germano Celant

It is on the stage of the 'everyday', of the world and of the things and objects in the world, that the self, through the processes of its imagination, gambles with constructing an 'alternative' to the world, a history and identity of its own. The self is constantly confronted with the irrepressible oscillation of the things of the world, and risks getting lost in the labyrinth of their infinite travels. In order to avoid that loss, and to face down the terror of being drowned in the world's avalanche of objects, the self tries to capture some of these things, to make them its own; it gives them a personal value, whether positive or negative. In doing so, it wrenches them from the 'nonplace' of the mass of objects in the world, and brings them into a relationship with itself; it creates a mould, a double, which represents it. In art, the consequences of this appropriation have been mimesis and representation. Both create doubles, formulations defined, now sympathetically, now negatively, in terms of the original thing. All of the different historical avant-garde, subtle variations on the double, the infinitesimal similarities and differences they set up between the double and the object or thing it repeats, as with Marcel Duchamp, for example, constitute a reinterpretation of it, a more perfected attempt to match, to 'see', in poker terms, the stakes laid out on the table of everyday things.

The attempt to reveal the cards of the everyday allows the double a fluctuating meaning in the imagination, a latent force capable of eradicating the limits and boundaries of the object. The double becomes an explosive irradiating energy, setting the mirage of objects adrift. This permits the self to emerge from its uncertainty and to establish the coordinates of a net of references, a grid into which things can be made to fall. This network full of objects serves as a map, which can be used to retraverse and to reinhabit the world. It is on this map that the artist marks out and sketches in the 'known'. He or she moves along its meridians and parallels, gaining an awareness of its geography from voyages and landings on the slippery coasts of its different islands, its different objects. One might also consider the artists' awareness as a line through time, a course connecting the various islands of the archipelago, a mobile sign, a boat or hull with, loaded on board, all the data that the self produces, gathers and manifests as it passes from thing to thing, from island to island. It is with words and thoughts, images and objects, that the artist self tries to find its way.

This book by Claes Oldenburg and Coosje van Bruggen begins, on the cover, with an archipelago of islands surrounded by the sea upon which floats a *Bottle of Notes*, following courses set by the imagination. This cover is a 'preliminary totality', introducing the internal logic of the book as well as its contents. It is a navigational guide to the exploration of the archipelago of islands and atolls that follows in the form of notebook pages and images of the models for colossal monuments. If the symbolic space of the map is the condition for a genesis of awareness, for Claes and Coosje the space is delimited by the challenging boundaries of images, objects and words. On these beaches and cliffs, all voyages of knowledge must attempt to land, often beside the shipwrecked remains of other attempts.

The map presents the sense of a world that Claes and Coosje want to confer on 'things'. It organises a universe of 'islands' based on their projects, the *Three-Way Plug*, the *Toothbrush*, the *Screwarch*, the *Match*, the *Piano*, the *Pencil*. It gives these things concreteness and legibility, investing the objects with a permanence that metaphorically makes them visitable territories, even if still absent and remote. Claes and Coosje have created a web of real references in their imagination. This plan to hypothesize a region that represents the modern era of objects may seem like a nonsense device, but, in a 'transgressive' sense, it has a certain logic: unexpectedly, it creates a system out of absurd and uncontrollable meanings. Such an interest in the absurd has produced high artistic expressions in the past, from Alfred Jarry's science of pataphysics and Jonathan Swift's *Gulliver's Travels*, to the urban landscapes of Giorgio de Chirico.

Considerations such as these help us to understand how the *Bottle of Notes* is intended. It is a container that takes its form from writing. Metaphorically, the bottle is the 'bridge', the link between the various lands, and between Claes and Coosje. It is the body of human knowledge that the navigator trusts against the unknown, against inclement weather and the currents of cause and effect that intervene in the study and analysis of the real world. It is a thought encased in an object. A bottle may be storm-tossed and reeling, yet it almost always manages to save itself and reach a beach, a place in which to disclose its message. It floats and slides along the waves on a journey in which it becomes an instrument of communication between two beings, or between two cultures. It has a transparency that allows one to perceive the doubleness of its existence. It is an interstice between inside and out, unconscious and conscious, personal and public, nonsense and sense. In the terms of Duchamp's *Large Glass*, it is a *Small Glass* that seeks, like a primitive alembic, to define the primary requirements of seeing and understanding, between the polarities of the masculine and the feminine.

As an object in and of itself, the *Bottle of Notes* is made up of handwriting and signs. It is born of the encounter between drawing, writing and sculpture, which it shows to be intimately allied, reciprocal through interpenetration, in unity. Underlying it is a symbiosis between artist and writer, Claes and Coosje, no longer juxtaposed but coexisting in a sort of suspension: the making of icons is an inversion of linguistic creation, and vice versa. The identities of artist and writer are presented in an absolutely unified relationship; the tools of communicating in both writing and sculpting are presented on the same plane. They become one. And if the word is the transparent envelope of an idea, even more so can it be used in a plastic, visual sense, in the tradition of Mallarmé and of Apollinaire, of Futurism's free use of words, and of concrete poetry. In *Bottle of Notes*, words are a material substance that can be used to form images. By the same token, images make writing. The inertia and stasis of sculpture are overcome; art is pushed toward a simultaneity of action with poetry. The object that Claes and Coosje have designed tends to fuse the two, establishing a vital dialogue in which roles and functions are reversed. This symbiosis of artist and writer questions one's usual expectations of either role, expectations based on the traditional codes that require interpretations and messages, roles and functions, to be kept clear and distinct. What is proposed here is an integration of languages or persons seemingly orbiting irreconcilably, but actually spilling over, one into the other.

The vitreous quality of the *Bottle of Notes* sculpture reveals a bipolar structure, artist/writer, Claes/Coosje, in which everything is presented doubled and able to be doubled. Nothing has a clear identity; every term is ready to be overturned into another, to take on the look of its opposite. The bottle is invoked as a mooring place, a hinge where opposites converge, the necessary point of cohesion where the thinking *and the seeing*, the emotional and the logical, the rational and the irrational, the drawing and the word, the masculine and the feminine of the writer and the artist are established as a compact and brilliant figure, full of meaning. In this sense, creation becomes an oscillation between poles. The space within whose perimeter the transmutation and interchange between parts takes place is the space of creativity. This doubling is the reason why the names of the island objects are presented mirrored and inverted, accompanied by their 'shadows'. Their identity is twofold, inflecting a 'one' that is in reality a 'two', where 'screw' becomes 'wercs', 'toothbrush' 'hsurbhtoot'. Two sets of opposite terms, the concrete name of an object, and its incomprehensible double, confront one another. The copresence of both meaningful and meaningless names makes it clear that Claes and Coosje, our two explorers, have made a map of a Land of the Double, a Land of the Echo. The messages they have entrusted to their bottle move about between a concrete world (screw, toothbrush, three-way plug) and its unknown and, for now, unknowable reflection (wercs, hsurbhtoot, gulp-yaw-eerht). Their double use of words designates a world overturned, a reversal of the perspectives of top and bottom, large and small.

It shouldn't be surprising, then, that since the 1960s Oldenburg's work has often invoked Swift's *Travels into Several Remote Nations of the World by Lemule Gulliver*, 1726, the well-known tale of an ingenuous voyager's visits to a series of nations with indecipherable names, inhabited by populations of different cultures and physical sizes. Gulliver is a prototype of the fictional hero who, like the bottle, navigates through unknown lands. The realities of the different societies with which he comes in contact are always exaggerated, thus functioning for Swift as ironic, parodistic allegories of his own world. Claes and Coosje have adopted the same process. They seek to follow Gulliver's journey from beginning to end, from Lilliput to Brobdingnag, that is, from the sketchbook notes through the models to the colossal monuments. While so doing, they furnish a satirical and critical interpretation of everyday contemporary life. As with Swift, one way they do this is through the metaphoric use of magnifying glasses. They magnify an object with a specific correspondence or assonance in history or memory, in the context of the culture in which it will be located. This hyperbole has an iconoclastic charge which they exploit to the maximum, creating confusion and disorder. The colossal monuments comprehend the worlds of both Lilliput and Brobdingnag, the micro and the macro. Their visual qualities, expanded by the enlarging lens, become instruments of hyperbolic upheaval. They create a reality where 'monstrosity' lurks behind the common object, in the Latin sense of *monstrum* as 'marvel'. The hyperbolic marvellousness of the sculptures of Claes Oldenburg and Coosje van Bruggen creates an imaginary world where objects become occasions of confrontation. In 'The Voyage to Lilliput', the account of the contents of Gulliver's pockets reveals a deep rift between Gulliver's perceptions and those of the Liliputians; similarly, the objects of these sculptures, translated from the language of the real world into that of art, reveal the violence and strangeness of reality.

Like Gulliver, Oldenburg loves to catalogue things. His texts and lists are long samplings of words and objects. The ruling criteria of his selections are

Cover for Bottle of Notes
and Some Voyages, Version One
1987
Watercolour, felt pen
26 × 40½ in (66 × 103 cm)

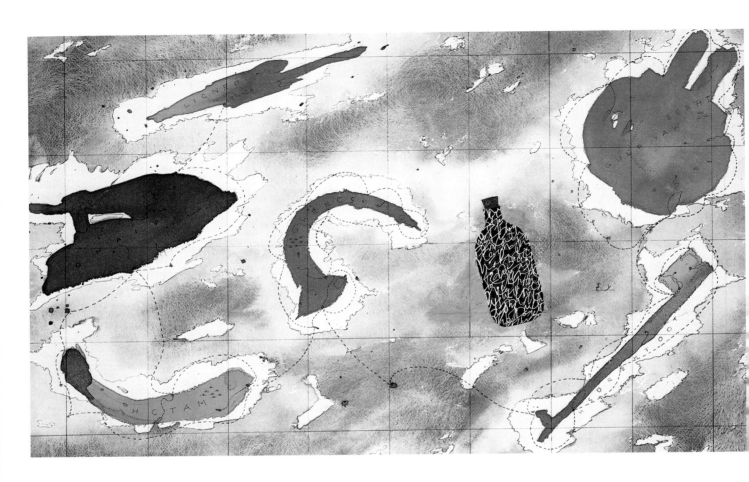

both aesthetic and fantastic. They are free in their approach, ignoring the taboos imposed by the usual linguistic codes. In mimicking a philosophical stance, they deal great blows to the contemporary contemplative ideal, still conceived in terms of order and tradition. For Oldenburg, as Gulliver, the object is a metaphor, with multiple meanings, at the very least, the kind of double meaning implicit in 'screw/wercs'. Thus the object acts as a sign of the behaviour of a given culture, whether in Mildendo or Middlesbrough, Lolbrulgrud or Los Angeles, Lagado or Venice. Every object will reveal something about a place's inhabitants and about their languages.

Once linguistic terms are made relative, the relationships between word and thing becomes problematic. Objective notions about the order of things can no longer be proposed. Thus an equivalent between the existing world and the sphere of language becomes possible. As Gulliver says, 'Words are only names for things'. The only valid proposal for communicating, then, would be the proposal by the Academy of Lagado to do away with words entirely and to discourse through things themselves:

'However, many of the most learned and wise adhere to the new scheme of expressing themselves by things, which hath only this inconvenience attending it, that if a man's business be very great, and of various kinds, he must be obliged in proportion to carry a greater bundle of things upon his back, unless he can afford one or two strong servants to attend him. I have often beheld two of those sages almost sinking under the weight of their packs, like peddlars among us; who when they met in the streets, would lay down their loads, open their sacks, and hold conversation for an hour together; then put up their implements, help each other to resume their burthens, and take their leave. But for short conversations a man may carry simple implements in his pockets and under his arms, enough to supply him, and in his house he cannot be at a loss. Therefore the room where company meet who practise this art, is full of all things ready at hand, requisite to furnish matter for this kind of artificial converse. Another great advantage proposed by this invention was that it would serve as an universal language to be understood in all civilised nations, whose goods and utensils are generally of the same kind, or nearly resembling, so that their uses might easily be comprehended.'

This passage, quoted by Oldenburg in the catalogue to his exhibition at the Sidney Janis Gallery, New York, in 1966, establishes his interest in skipping over any mediation between word and thing, favouring the latter. His idea is to overturn the positions of science and ordinary sense in order to facilitate visions that are simple, essential and definite, as opposed to the redundancy and surfeit of the frantic signs in abstract discourse. For Oldenburg as for Swift, illiteracy paradoxically becomes the line of defence for language and letters, in a word, for culture, against new sages and the schemes of rationalization they propose.

The useful aspect of the project Swift describes is that it gives literal weight to the word. However, it also risks a situation in which the relationships between various countries or islands, between various cultures, would be realized through a language made up only of 'goods and utensils'. This would mean a levelling of cultural differences, but would also restrict human intercourse to nothing more than the results of material production, to commodities, and the tools used to produce them. The Oldenburgs' *Bottle of Notes* sculpture seeks to avoid this danger. It closes a perfect circle: in its symbiosis of sculpture and writing, it proposes a strict metaphoric collaboration between word and body. From this point of view, the sculptural bottle wants, as Viktor Sklovskij would say, to transmit the impression of the object as 'vision', not as recognition. It is a project and a model in a fantastic key, capable of fabulous future developments. It indicates a path neither defined nor resolved, open to all events.

But *Bottle of Notes* is the metaphoric title of the book as well as of Claes's and Coosje's project for Middlesbrough. The book contains an anthology of about twenty years' worth of sketchbook notes and projects, and of images of the models and maquettes for colossal monuments; the pages are turned as in a logbook, with maps of every possible configuration outlining imaginery continents, islands and seas which seek and sometimes find a concrete topology. Thus *Bottle of Notes*, like *Gulliver's Travels*, performs a documentary function and follows a particular order. Given the parodistic function of its data and its coordinates, however, it is a catalogue of an ironic, critical kind. It speaks of a rationally ordered world, but it is based on a 'rupture' of the order of things, a plundering of reality by art. What takes shape is a universe out of *The Thousand and One Nights*. Sinbad the sailor is replaced by Claes and Coosje. 'Fish 100 and 200 cubits long', and 'serpents so thick and long that each one could swallow an elephant', are replaced by buildings in the form of letters, a teddy bear, a pair of scissors, or a three-way plug; by bridges in the form of a saw or a screw, by a library built like a pencil, by fountains in the shape of a drill or an orange juicer, by toast cathedrals, butter beach-houses, and a piano hammock. The process of sticking words together, of freely combining them, is supported by the sculptures themselves, which end up 'signifying' what their titles say. Thus a piano-hammock is a strange symbiosis between a piano and a hammock, and the screwarch envisions a metamorphosis of the span of a bridge in Rotterdam into enormous screws. In actual fact, 'words are only names for things'.

Having paged through the entire book *A Bottle of Notes*, one discovers that its title takes literal shape in the project for Middlesbrough. Here is delineated a potential colossal monument, a fantastic evocation of a scenario relating to another explorer, Captain Cook, a protagonist in the history of the Middlesbrough area. Above all the bottle is a container, recalling both a ship and a floating vase. It thus refers to the tradition of the port, and to an English citizen who, in 1830, became famous for his Pottery Farm as well as for his shipbuilding yard. The bottle also reveals meanings tied to Captain Cook, in the phrase that form its transparent shell. The phrase on the exterior reads, 'we had every advantage we could desire in observing the whole of the passage of the planet Venus over the sun's disc'; and the one on the interior, 'I like to remember seagulls in full flight gliding over the ring of canals'. These phrases reflect the identities of the explorers, as well as their relationship to the story of Captain Cook. The first phrase seems formulated by the explorer Claes, who transmutes the energy of Venus, that is, of the feminine, in the crucible of images. The sentence is taken from the log of Cook's first exploratory voyage, in 1768, when he embarked from Plymouth and landed in New Zealand. The phrase of the other explorer, Coosje, refers not to a specific goal, means or figure, but to a more romantic concern with nature in the form of seagulls. The birds are associated with memories of the pleasure and freedom of youth, and with the canals of both Amsterdam and Venice

The fusion of each sentence with the other is a fusion in which opposites are dissolved, and both images and words become, to quote Gulliver, 'bodies of much weight and gravity'.

For now, the sculptural *Bottle of Notes* is in a design stage, a vehicle for the desire to build a large-scale project in Middlesbrough. Thus it is still sailing on the high seas; it has not yet reached port. It seeks to make visible the invisible, as an idol makes visible a god. It hypothesizes a possibility beyond the usual boundaries; it prefigures the unimaginable. Like all models and prototypes, it moves in advance of what it embodies. But what in fact is a model in art, and what is its history, from yesterday to today, from Kasimir Malevich to Oldenburg?

To use a dictionary definition, the model and the maquette are 'reproductions, in reduced scale, of a planned work, executed in order to study and experiment'. They have been used as such throughout the history of art and architecture. The model represents a methodical attempt to open a space, to set a stage in the world of hypotheses and dreams. It is an essential scanning device for exploring the creation of architecture and aesthetic volume in the city. It is by definition an intermediate rather than a final product, simulating the thing desired before it is actually made. The model is a moment in a process, a means for hastening into being, in visual and tactile terms, a 'motif', a thematic, plastic, visual structure of the work to come. It is a first step toward an event; infinite variables depart from it. The result of manipulations, assemblings, gluings, it reflects the pleasure that lies in expectation of the real object. It determines whether or not a certain effect is actually possible, and therefore is located at the intersection between desire and research.

The model requires interpretation as a site unto itself, an assembly point for the signs or symptoms of a flow of thought that will eventually be given order and definition. If it functions as a look into the future, and as a look into an imaginary, utopian, as yet placeless topography, it becomes a privileged signifier, summarizing the unstable, aleatory meanings of a specific sensibility and thought process. The model is a zone of suspension, half way between the sculpture and architecture that will form the real landscape. Here, words become confused, and end up creating a simulated panorama of the imaginary. The model can combine elements and signs in ways impossible in the world at large. At least in theory, it can produce a fantastic order of the real.

From the beginning of the century on, the historical avant-garde, using such opportune techniques as collage and bricolage, sought to free the model or maquette from its role as the promise of an object or architecture waiting to be realised. They sought to confer on the model an autonomous poetic and artistic value. The intent was to consider the model or maquette not as a 'mechanism of passage from one form to the other', but as an energetic and eloquent statement on its own. This change of meaning tended to bring out the similarities between the various creative languages, lessening the distances between them. A twist in proportions pushed the perverse, intimate creative project, in whatever field, into an equivalent to or at least a correspondence to the element of urban scale. For the Futurists as for the Surrealists, the 'reasons' behind the dynamic and profound discourse of art lay in the criss-crossing movements and events of the city. Accordingly, all the forms and texts realised in painting and sculpture, literature and cinema, music and architecture, became manifestations of the metropolitan theatre. They were offered as 'metaphors' of streets and buildings, neighbourhoods and industrial landscapes, and they were meant to be true explorations of everyday life. To produce a piece of sculpture or a poem was to hypothesize an imaginary field of the urban environment. The search for a commonality between creativity and the metropolis was encouraged by the Cubist incorporation of everyday objects and object fragments, things drawn from the banal urban context, within the space of the painting, beginning in 1912–13. The process reached its absolute form in 1917, when Duchamp raised the readymade to the dignity of art. Thus a bottle rack, just like a skyscraper, became an instrument of art, and likewise art became a poeticization of the urban environment.

Once the threshold determining the borders between art and architecture had been crossed, the differences between origination and reproduction, imaginary and real, prototype and realization, genuine and copy, design and execution, model and building, became speculative. These hitherto separate categories came to reflect images, one the double of the other. The model had been an object 'outside' art and architecture, in grey and neutral exile, without value; now it was used to design the imaginary. But it was with Constructivism that this amalgamation of polarities developed in a positive sense toward a visual research and a practical form. In the course of the few years between 1915 and 1920, both Malevich and Vladimir Tatlin sought to emancipate sculpture in the direction of 'spatial construction'. Malevich's models for the 'Architectons', and Tatlin's for the *Monument to the Third International*, are hypotheses for the dialectical resolution of these antitheses.

Applying the methods of Suprematist painting to the development of volumes in space, and beginning with his 'Planits' of 1915–16, Malevich realized a series of maquettes, first in cardboard (1920–21), then in plaster (1922–23). These 'Architectons' develop the projection of the black square

Kazimir S. Malevich, *Planit*
1923–27
From: *Malévitch. Architectones, peintures, dessins*, Paris, 1980

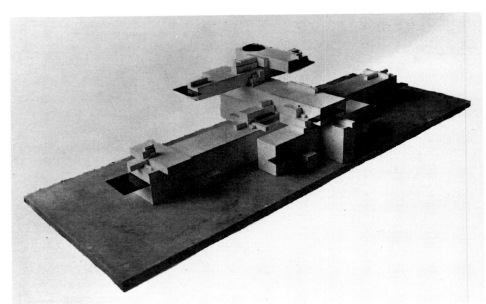

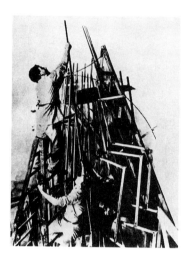

Two pictures of construction of the monument to the III International (1920). In the second picture, from left to right: Dimisich-Tolstaia, Tatlin, Sapiro, Mejerzon From: Larisza A. Zsadova, *Tatlin*, Budapest

into space. They are volumes born of a serial proliferation, both vertical and horizontal, of cubes and parallelepipeds. Varying in height and extension, the 'Architectons' seek a dynamic with which to explore the 'cosmic dimension of Suprematism', a stratospheric depth symbolized by the use of white plaster, an element suggesting both construction and an awareness of the world. Malevich's Suprematist maquettes are models not only in the concrete sense, but theoretically as well. Through their perfection of execution and the clarity of their light-reflecting material, they seek to 'crystallize', as though the Suprematist oracle had thought to build a synthesis between the imaginary and the real. Even though they render material a possible trajectory of pure forms, their existence as prototypes must always retain for them an 'immaterial' presence, that of both the secular and the spirit light that shine on and through society. In addition, the orthogonal cross format to which the inert matter is adapted is a sign of passage and transit from the obscure to the illuminated, from the unformed to the elementary form, a passage that can be achieved only through a synthesis between high and low, celestial and terrestrial. The maquettes, shown first in Vitebsk in 1920–21 and then in 1926 in Leningrad, are 'sculptures' that, through their luminosity and perfection, are meant to serve as an alphabet in the creation of the language of contemporaneity. (Their titles are actually *Alfa, Beta, Zeta*.)

Tatlin's model for the *Monument to the Third International* establishes a dynamic, energetic canon in which the exemplary figures of Euclidean geometry are set at the centre and their means of construction and support at the periphery. Tatlin imagines the utopian dream as an intertwining of moments no longer compact, but interspersing solids and voids. It is primarily the result of 'montage'. This is a construction based both on materials and on human action, as documented in the photographs of the realization of the first model in 1920. Presented in what was then Petrograd (and today Leningrad), the work emerges from a collective labour whose end is the achievement of both an ideal site and a 'model' for that site, which takes concrete form. The construction of the maquette for the *Monument to the Third International* in 1919 thus reflects a group of meanings; it advances the principles and foundations of a here-and-now that is meant to become an elsewhere-and-future. Beginning in the 1920s, the intuition that the model can serve to capture the 'germination', the true creative process before the elaboration of the details, is transferred into a generalized creative practice. Ilia Chashnik, Ivan Leonidov and Gustav Klucis put this to the test with their maquettes of three-dimensional constructions and of buildings and radio kiosks. These maquettes combine plaster and wood, cardboard and glass, materials here left in the rough, there painted; they translate a materialist vision that only the everyday object, with its inexpressiveness and non-subjectivity, succeeds in communicating.

In their materials, methods of execution and paintwork, the models for Theo van Doesburg's *Haus eines Kunstlers*, 1923, and *Haus Meudon*, 1929, show that he perceives a need for lightness and transparency in this part of his work, almost as though the miniaturized vision of his neoplastic 'archi-sculptures' is meant to lead to the definition of an abstract void. At the same time, the absence of depth, and the modularity of the thin cardboard surfaces, indicate constructions based both horizontally and vertically on equilibrium and on the multiple use of weights, planes, volumes and colours. The effect

Kurt Schwitters
Haus Merz
1920
From: John Elderfield, *Kurt Schwitters*
London, 1985

Kurt Schwitters
Schloss und Kathedrale mit Hofbrunnen
1922
From: John Elderfield, *Kurt Schwitters*
London, 1985

of instability that one perceives in the De Stijl models, in contrast to the monolithic quality of Malevich's 'Architectons', is in fact created by the multiple interchangeable properties of the modules used. These are light and movable, and are capable of entering a complex circuit of exchanges of forms and of identities, as in a game of cards. The same impulses toward a primary, elementary elaboration govern the maquettes for Georges Vantongerloo's *Airport*, 1928, made of silver-plated copper, and for Jean Groin's *Structures of the Spatial House*, 1930. Following the dictates of Neoplasticism, these models push 'natural and abstract reality' to coexist, to achieve the 'absolute solemnity of forms'. For these artists as for Piet Mondrian, painting and sculpture are a stage toward architecture, and the maquette is the configuration of a possible way of being. On the horizon is a model of existence that can flow into the productive sphere, with Tatlin and van Doesburg, or that can remain in utopian territory, inscribing itself unhindered within the space of the Other History, as with Malevich and Mondrian.

To compose the imaginary only according to a syntactic and abstract order of forms and figures is to establish a discourse that excludes the banal and the ephemeral. In the Russian and Dutch *avant-gardes*, in fact, the 'ruined' codes of history and of the present are refuted; codes are sought in the new, in the future. The system invoked does not mimic objective reality. The Dadaists depart from the same premise, but they arrive at the opposite working process: they debase the architectural model or maquette through the introduction of found materials. Their goal is to break with old linguistic habits, to negate old conventions and academic dogmas. The Dadaists' dislocation techniques create a paradise in which every object and every sign becomes something different. They too want to reform art, to establish it as a new language, but the multimaterial collages of Marcel Janco, Kurt Schwitters, Max Ernst and Raoul Hausmann preach an 'awareness of objects and of their sensory fabric'. The Dadaist vision of the model is entirely conditioned by this message. The selection of materials for the model and the method of its assemblage are based not on the idea of the prototype, but on the found object. The goal is to produce effects as well as to convey ideas. The Schwitters maquettes *Haus Merz*, 1920, and *Schloss und Kathedrale mit Hofbrunnen*, 1923, convey a continuous aleatory state, and a confusion of traces of the stages in their production. With the introduction of small wheels, toys, buttons, and the bottoms of boxes, the formative rules of architectural discourse are disoriented by associations of play and chance, of irony and frivolity. These inclusions reflect not only a social critique, but also a desire for the unpredictable. The fortuitous encounter of the house-machine with the tower-toy and the button-window eludes all previous definitions of architectural identity, breaking the logic of normal experience.

Abandoning the usual equivalences between object and architecture, the 'nonmeaning' of the Dadaist maquettes not only implies a parody of the usual process of design but also promotes a secondary effect, a recuperation of the 'real'. Recomposing fragments and residues of the everyday with no concern for logic but a visual one, these maquettes escape the logic of use, with its maturity and balance, to disseminate pleasure instead. The image no longer seeks resolution and finality of form, but suggests a rupture, a dislocation. It separates itself from all concerns for aesthetic and linguistic order. The Dadaist assemblages are chance configurations, hypotheses of a construction 'outside reason'. Their presence is 'diabolical', scandalous, oneiric; they suggest whole new architectures, not yet legitimate, and unable to claim a history in the world unless it be that of banality. It is as if the making of a model were invested with a different attitude and thought process from those of the later construction, as if the very practice of assembling and gluing, manipulating and fitting, implied the play of desire.

This sensual and sensory energy, together with Dadaism's iconoclastic charm, are dissolved in the pleasure of looking at the object when it becomes a flesh and blood 'character', soft and tender, in the sculptures of Claes Oldenburg. Oldenburg's process may recall the Dadaist and Surrealist interest in extracting certain objects from the homogeneous expanse of the everyday and inserting them into an art context, but his approach is decidedly broader. The object extracted is not considered a generic image of the world, an element to be absorbed within a collage of other pictorial or sculptural elements. Instead, it is exalted for its own identity, for the charm and distinction that differentiate it from other things. Furthermore, Oldenburg, to obtain this 'personalization' of the object, does not 'humiliate' it, distorting it in function or in name as Duchamp did. Rather, he exalts it in its most absolute singularity. He erects a monument to its identity, which, as in the best psychological literature, is always fragile, vulnerable, hidden. The obviousness of the everyday is transformed into illumination, into something

Theo van Doesburg, C. van Eesteren
Model of an Artist's House
Paris, 1923
on, mirror, steel, aluminum

Free Stamp, Model, Lying Version
1987
Cast epoxy
3¼ × 5½ × 2¼ in (8.2 × 14 × 5.7 cm)

The fifteen-metre *Free Stamp* was to stand upright on a 'pad' in front of the new Standard Oil building in central Cleveland, Ohio. After completion of the sculpture in 1986, its installation was blocked when British Petroleum took over Standard Oil, replaced its management and broke the contract with the artists. The lying version is a reformulation of the subject for an alternative site in a park beside the Cleveland City Hall. The model shows an unpainted version of the work.

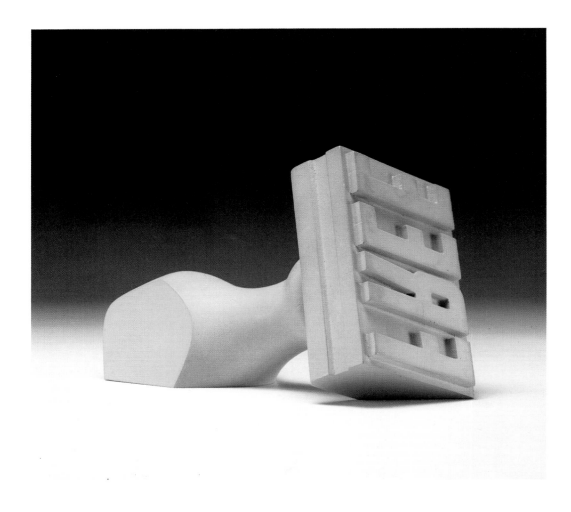

oonbridge and Cherry, Model
87
ood, plexiglass, painted
½ × 22½ × 49½ in
7.2 × 57.2 × 125.7 cm)

The *Spoonbridge and Cherry* fountain, due to be installed in April 1988, is the centerpiece of a sculpture garden in front of the Walker Art Center in Minneapolis. The bowl of the *Spoonbridge* rests on an island in a pond. In summer, a mist will be projected from the end of the stem, while water issues from its base, surrounding the 'cherry' and draining into the bowl and pond.

Notebook Page: Studies for
Lipstick Ascending
1969
Ball-point pen, felt pen, crayon
Four sheets, each 5 × 2¾ in (12.7 × 7 cm)
on sheet 11 × 8½ in (28 × 21.6 cm)

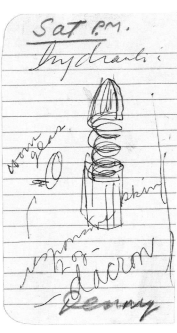

disconcerting, as if to 'exorcise' the experience of confrontation with the world's objects. The work is an attempt to restore to visual language meaningfulness that has been erased by the alienation and abstraction of the everyday object, and to do so by making the object itself burst on the scene as a vivid character. Illuminating or, better, casting light upon this sphinx called a thing, Oldenburg extracts from the flow of the everyday a screw, a button, a light switch, a hat, a flashlight, a cigarette butt, and so forth, and brings out their enigma. He lets the unexpected, the startling, the fantastic, the foolish break through.

From 1969 on, Oldenburg's work operates on two levels: setting in view the reified and amplified object, he criticizes the language of mass culture, but at the same time he deconstructs this same language with his magnifying glass. Focusing on collective icons, on apparently banal objects and usages, he makes them tangible, soft, penetrable, and thus reconcilable with the human. This reconciliation, even if it has a critical dimension, lays the foundation of a design process in which the object is the great imaginative force, the well of an intellectual energy that lives off the surrealness of the everyday, and that can use a semiotic deconstruction of the object to oppose the closed, suffocating system in which the object exists. This operation opens up a new territory where the object moves from mere instrumentality into becoming the metaphor of a great iconoclastic humour. It becomes the protagonist of a long novel, in which it undertakes extravagant, impossible exploits. A true story emerges in which the object acquires dimension and variations that carry it into every linguistic, formal and material zone. It draws on all the senses; it overcomes its limits and its relative immobility, materializing with felicitous ease in design, sculpture and architecture. It is born and reborn in different realms, repeating itself through a variety of different existences in terms of material (paper=steel=cloth), function (plug=building=balloon), scale (large=small, distant=close), number (many=one). As Oldenburg describes it in 'Log of the Three-Way Plug', the sequence of experimentation is in three stages. The number three is the symbol of harmony and proportion, and expresses the search for a perfect synthesis between the intellectual, the cosmic and the human; it also manifests the conceptual destination of the research. The triangle of paper, steel and cloth expresses the passage of Coosje van Bruggen's and Claes Oldenburg's working process from writing on paper, with its reflection of pure consciousness, to concrete transformation into metal and cloth. The metal is a sign of robustness and duration, of rigidity and permanence, while the cloth indicates lightness, flexibility and impermanence, and thus bears a relation to the life of the body. These material definitions are often united in Claes and Coosje's writing by an 'equals' sign (=), a bridge that allows the artists to pass freely from one zone to the other. Furthermore, this kind of passage between materials recalls the initiatory alchemic voyage of the shaman engaged in personal transmutations. Thus what is public is also private, and vice versa.

As one can see from the complexity of these processes, for Claes and Coosje the dynamic of critical and visual thought is many-layered, grinding forms together with inexhaustible energy. In this sense, the triad 'plug=building=balloon' implies the inextinguishability of any subject that can be transformed from a manageable object for personal use into an architectural form

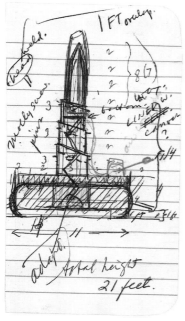

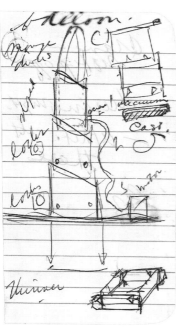

or an airborne artifact, and back again. Human, terrestrial and celestial connotations are always interchangeable and equivalent. And the equivalences of scale and number, large=small, distant=close, many=one, that embellish the passages from low to high, from natural to artificial, and so forth open up further meanings. The work contains within itself a discussion of elevation and scale, of dimension and vision; in fact, as Oldenburg writes, 'The colossal-monument proposals have to be very precise as to scale, one has to see at a glance (as one glances at a car or building) just how big the thing proposed is. This is entirely done by comparison. Precision of viewpoint, suggestion of atmosphere also help but, most important is an imagination convinced of the existence of what the hand sets down'. The work of art thus sees the actualization of all possible poetic and pragmatic forces. It has no fear of becoming lost in the brilliance of words, with Coosje, or in the sensual language of images, with Claes. The object dances from one state to another, from text to sketch to model to sculpture to large-scale project. It is the wellspring of thought; its unifying power allows it a permanent vitality. This is why the notebook pages and the models or maquettes shown in this book, as well as the theoretical passages, are as important as the larger finished works. They are already projects in themselves, 'real' plastic creations with their own value and meaning.

Proposal for a Monument to the Survival of the University of El Salvador, Blasted Pencil (Which Still Writes), 1983, demonstrates the long route that Oldenburg has taken since his early works in the 1960s. Then, he saw the everyday object in its enigmatic nature as an icon of a culture, its life contingent and ephemeral, ruled by the laws of products and commodities. Metaphorically, he sought through his sculptures to halt the senseless and crazy proliferation of objects made to become obsolete and to be replaced, sought to historicize portions of the output by removing them from circulation and making them 'astounding', or revealing them as such. Then, during the 1970s, working with van Bruggen, Oldenburg gave up the illusion of being able to resist the ever accelerating procedures of industry and the market, and turned to exploring the 'obscene' innards of reality. The work took on a more ideological, political dimension. This is the period of the 'critical' metamorphosis represented by the large-scale projects. Their complexity, of facture, logistics, bureaucracy, financing and so forth, reduces the spontaneity involved in the creation of the earlier soft sculptures, but these works greatly amplify the viewer's perception of and insight into the excess of urban modernity.

In looking at *Blasted Pencil*, for example, one can see a coming and going between life and death, or between pride and shame, if the viewer is American. Coosje's text documenting the tragic recent past of El Salvador, accompanied by a drawing by Claes that is abstract and hard of line, together resemble a sharp cry, the kind that can end in silence. Another drawing shows the 'pencil' surrounded by a large black field, as if it were the victim of isolation and loss. The black, of course, is a sign of death, and, politically, it is the hue of fascism. The same sense of loss, not of images but of people, marks van Bruggen's writing. It is as if the drawing and writing for this project sought to reflect the fragility of El Salvador's intellectual life, which runs the risk of being rubbed out at the same time that it strains in agony to survive. The work recognises both the broken body of intellectual discourse in El

Lipsticks in Piccadilly Circus,
London
1966
Postcard, clipping on paper
10 × 8 in (25.4 × 20.3 cm)
Collection: The Tate Gallery, London

Piccadilly Circus, London

ET 2087R

Lipstick mm.

Oldenburg 1966.

*Notebook Page: Studies for
Lipstick Ascending, 'TATLIN'
1969
Two of six sheets, various sizes
from sheet 11 × 8½ in (28 × 21.6 cm)*

*Notebook Page: Studies for
Lipstick Ascending*
1969
Pencil, crayon, ball-point pen, felt pen
11 × 8½ in (28 × 21.6 cm)

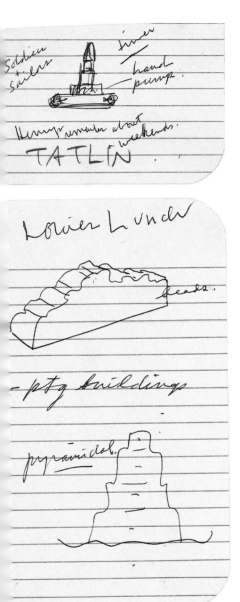

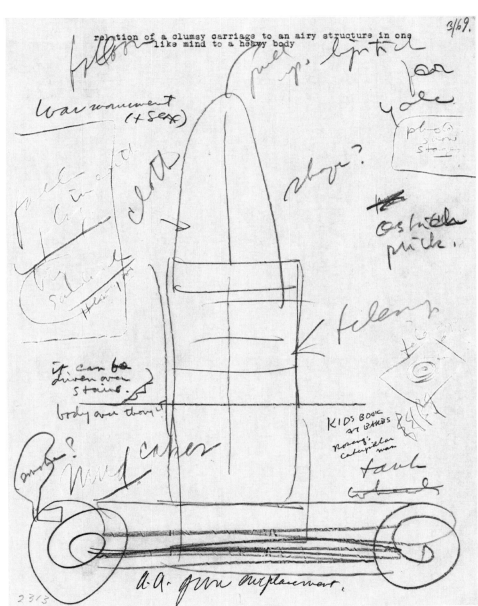

Study for Feasible Monument: Lipstick, Yale
1969
Pencil and spray enamel on paper
16¼ × 10¾ in (41.5 × 27.6 cm)

Lipstick, Ascending, on Caterpillar Tracks,
Fabrication Model
1969
Plaster, wood, cardboard, spray enamel
13 × 11 × 9⅞ in (33 × 39 × 25 cm)

Salvador and the sharpness of intellectual argument there. Politically, it offers the profile of a violent and thus ugly nature redeemed through intellectual comradeship. Terms usually dichotomous, nightmare and ecstasy, hallucination and consciousness, dream and wakefulness, apply equally to the art of Oldenburg and van Bruggen, for their work functions dichotomously, fluctuating always between levels: public and personal, conscious and unconscious, light and shadow, fire and water, masculine and feminine. It functions, it illuminates, through integrating parts usually separate from each other. It implies the necessity of a mixing, a fusion, of the most intimate fibres of the city, and of human beings.

To set one foot in the dark and one in the light, to stand on the threshold between them, is to capture the obscene everyday, which circulates freely between each realm. The everyday is everywhere; its objects saturate the eye without discretion or selection. In tripping up these objects as they circulate, in making them fall into the exceptional realm of art, Claes and Coosje create a short circuit. They make the senseless reasonable. And what is more senseless than a cigarette butt, a baked potato, a used match? These things are refuse, waste, consumed or dead, flaccid or broken. Yet Oldenburg and van Bruggen recover them, and create in them the potential for an intimate, personal, almost erotic relationship. Becoming lush and sensuous, these objects, reformed as models and large projects, touch down outside their original history and destiny, revealed in their fullness as beautiful stars of our secular public culture. And where does this magical transformation take place? In the language of art, which, returning to the metamorphoses of alchemy, changes brute into rare matter, into 'gold'. In all initiatory traditions transmutations of this kind are linked to fire, with its eternal transformative power. And it is fire that has consumed the match and the cigarette, and that has cooked the baked potato; it has depleted the object, robbed it of its firm shape. At the same time, however, in the tradition of the alchemist inventor, fire has also transmuted these perishable things. It has freed them from their ephemeral condition, given them immortality. Thus fire, like water, its principal opposite in magical initiatory procedures, contains both death and rebirth.

Fire, which both dissolves and absolves, resurrects the low and the banal, allows them to survive. It finds a correspondence in objects that use electricity: *English Light Switch, Three-Way Plug, Flashlight.* These things are tools for mediating, conducting, and regulating energy. Since their function is to translate that energy into usable form, light, the running of household appliances, they are also locations of consumption and transformation, passage and voyage, the intermediaries between open and closed, light and shadow. Thus these tools show that the dimension of the everyday is always a 'double' or a 'hinge' site, a doorway to hidden zones of life and energy. The breath of art can be drawn from the asphyxia of the everyday object. And just as the objects that Claes and Coosje choose are tied to the notion of transit, so the work of artist and writer is itself a journey through the languages and materials of sculpture and text, of construction and criticism. The consequence is a roaming within a heterogeneity of creative techniques, art and literature, architecture and theatre, to augment the tension and the circulation of aesthetic and critical energy. The work demonstrates an acceptance of the uncertain boundaries between these fields,

Lipstick, Ascending, on Caterpillar Tracks
1969
24 ft high (731.5 cm)
Sited 15 May 1969
Beinecke Plaza, Yale University

Lipstick, Ascending, on Caterpillar Tracks
1969

Standing Mitt with Ball
1973
Steel, lead and wood
12 ft high (365.8 cm)
Wave Hill, Bronx, New York

an interest in the points where they intersect, a rejection of the idea of their a priori exclusivity. Thus the cigarette butts can be seen in the form of *Colossal Fagends in Park Setting, with Man*, 1967, a proposal for Hyde Park, London, in which they lie about like fallen columns, or of *Fagends Carved in Rock*, 1972, where they become heroic towers cut into a mountainside, like the carvings on Mount Rushmore, or the colossal seated pharaohs in the Nile Valley. This latter proposal is a strange mixture of earth and landscape, of ancient statuary such as that of Easter Island and of newer realities, from 18th century cemeteries to modern electrical plants. Clearly, both art and industry produce 'residues', as cigarettes become discarded butts, the refuse of energetic consumption, now representing our culture. 'I think', Oldenburg states in *Six Themes*, in interview with Martin Friedman published by the Walker Art Center, Minneapolis in 1975, 'that an artist is somebody who makes symbolic statements on the condition of the universe. In one way or another, that's what I do'.

Art is born as an ephemeral encounter, a series of traces; it may survive centuries, but not without transformation and change of meaning. Everything in it is provisional, temporary. The recognition of art as such, however, is an integral part of the process of rupturing the old symbolic codes. Thus if Oldenburg and van Bruggen choose traditional objects in the culture to incorporate into art, it is not out of nostalgia for these things. Rather, it reflects an attempt to propose a continuity between things and languages, art and the everyday. The images encountering each other in Claes's and Coosje's work open up a clear awareness of the irresolvability of the dilemma between art and life, yet they also superimpose a vision of the marvellous upon the appearance of reality, to the point of integrating with it.

This text was translated from the Italian by Meg Shore and edited by David Frankel.

L.A.63.

1104

Notebook Pages

Facing page:
Notebook Page: Studies of a Circular Saw
Los Angeles, 1963
Watercolour, pencil, ball-point pen,
clippings
11 × 8½ in (28 × 21.6 cm)
The seductive representations of the *Circular
Saw* in the Sunday supplements direct this
super-tangible object towards painting as
well as sculpture. A larger drawing made
from this sketch shows the object gleaming in
deep space, like a planet or satellite.

Notebook Page: Study for an Outboard Motor in Action, on a Fragment of Stern with Notes on Technique and Materials
Paris, 1964
Ball-point pen, pencil, clippings
11 × 8½ in (28 × 21.6 cm)

An example of a single form made up of several objects and parts of objects.
The Sphinx, joined through photography to the Pyramid, is another. The parts not relevant to the configuration are scissored out, regardless of function, which is easy in the two dimensions of a clipping.

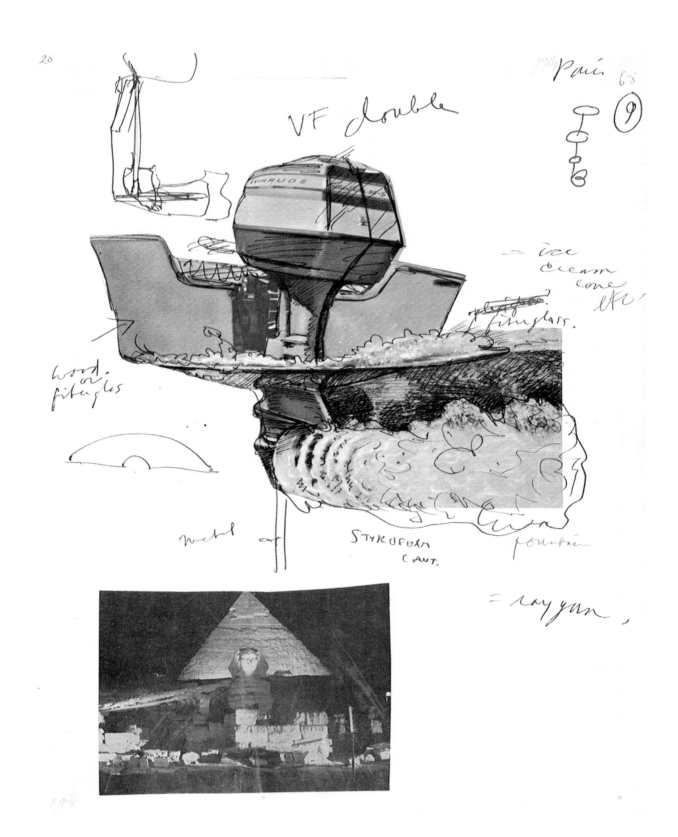

Notebook Page: Sphinx Compared to Screw
1970
Ball-point pen, felt pen
Sheet 5½ × 7⅝ in (13.3 × 19.3 cm)
and clipping 3 × 6¼ in (7.1 × 15.9 cm)
on sheet 11 × 8½ in (28 × 21.6 cm)

A drawing for a building on 57th Street, New York City, afterwards collaged together with the clipping of a screw. The Sphinx is derived from the trademark of a brand of typing paper.

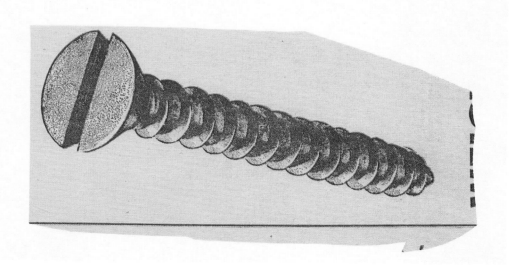

Notebook Page: Drill Bit in Place
of the Statue of Eros, 'extended'
London, 1966
Ball-point pen, felt pen, pencil,
clipping, postcard
Postcard 5½ × 3⅜ in (13.6 × 8.6 cm)
on sheet 10 × 8 in (25.4 × 20.3 cm)
on sheet 11 × 8½ in (28 × 21.6 cm)

The *Drill Bit* was probably suggested by the
circulation of traffic around the site.
It led to the proposal of a lipstick, the first use
of that subject, which brought Eros back in a
more contemporary form. Both *Drill Bit* and
Lipstick would rise and fall in relation to the
tide of the Thames river.

Notebook Page: Drill Bit in Place
of the Statue of Eros
London, 1966
Ball-point pen, pencil, clipping, postcard
Postcard 3½ × 5½ in (8.9 × 13.6 cm)
on sheet 10 × 8 in (25.4 × 20.3 cm)
on sheet 11 × 8½ in (28 × 21.6 cm)

London
66

V.d. blue

It goes up
and
down —

Notebook Page: Sliced Building,
Piccadilly Circus
London, 1966
Pencil, ball-point pen, crayon, watercolour
clipping, postcard
Sheet 10 × 8 in (25.4 × 20.3 cm)
on sheet 11 × 8½ in (28 × 21.6 cm)

The slicing knife is applied to a building
imagined to have the consistency of a cool
stick of butter or a pound cake. The knife
stays in, becoming part of the architecture.

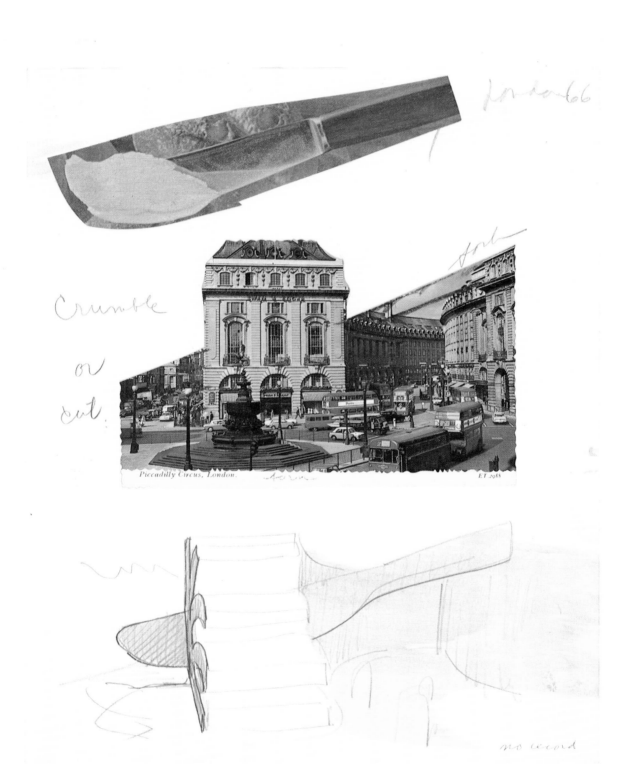

46

*Notebook Page: Proposal for a Building
in the Form of an Office Machine*
London, 1966
Ball-point pen, felt pen, pencil
and clipping on postcard
Postcard 5½ × 3½ in (14 × 8.2 cm)
on sheet 10 × 8 in (25.4 × 20.3 cm)
on sheet 11 × 8½ in (28 × 21.6 cm)

This addition to the 'New London', in its
ominous, unrelated scale, and technical,
rather than aesthetic, form, follows the
example of the Post Office Tower.

47

Notebook Page: Rear View Mirror in Place
of Nelson's Column, Trafalgar Square
London, 1966
Collage on clipping, pencil
5¼ × 6 in (13.5 × 15.2 cm)
on sheet 11 × 8½ in (28 × 21.6 cm)

'Rear view': the city looks at itself and at its
history. The same subject was proposed for
Chicago to stand on a pier in Lake Michigan,
extended from the city as if the city were the
body of a car.

Notebook Page: Square in London in the
Form of Objects on a Gentleman's
Night Table
London, 1966
Felt pen, watercolour, ball-point pen,
pencil, clipping
on sheet 10 × 8 in (25.4 × 20.3 cm)
on sheet 11 × 8½ in (28 × 21.6 cm)

An expensive watch, cufflinks and a lighter, a
carnation for the lapel, and enough money
in an elegant clasp, black, white, and gold
(favourite colours of London) resting on the
invitation which forms the boundaries of a
square. The watch-face could be a pool
which the hands of the watch slowly stir.

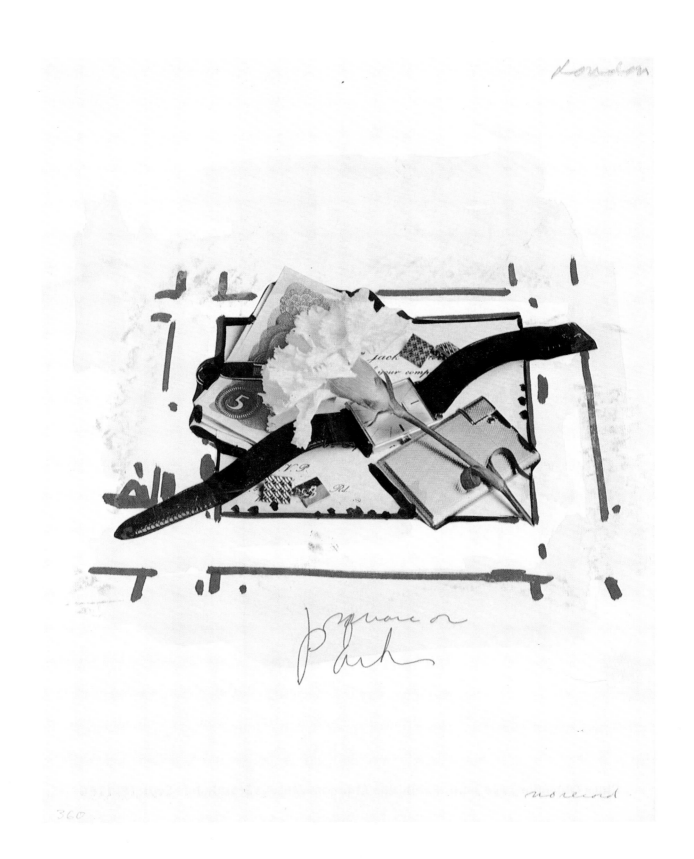

Notebook Page: Proposal for a Gearstick to Replace the Nelson Column, Trafalgar Square
London, 1966
Felt pen, crayon, watercolour
Postcard 5¼ × 3½ in (13.2 × 8.8 cm)
on sheet 11 × 8½ in (28 × 21.6 cm)

The gearstick version moves, popping in and out of gear positions, in a monumental imitation of the thousands of little gearstick motions all around the square.

50

Notebook Page: Study for the Fabrication
of the Soft Drum Pedal
1967
Pencil, felt pen, ball-point pen
11 × 8½ in (28 × 21.6 cm)

The reduction of a drum set to a sculpture
was a lengthy process which began with a
series of drawings simplifying and defining
the forms and details, followed by plans and
illustrated instructions for fabrication, of
which this is one. The word 'Red' does not
refer to the colour but is the nickname of a
carpenter, who would be assigned the pieces
marked with his name.

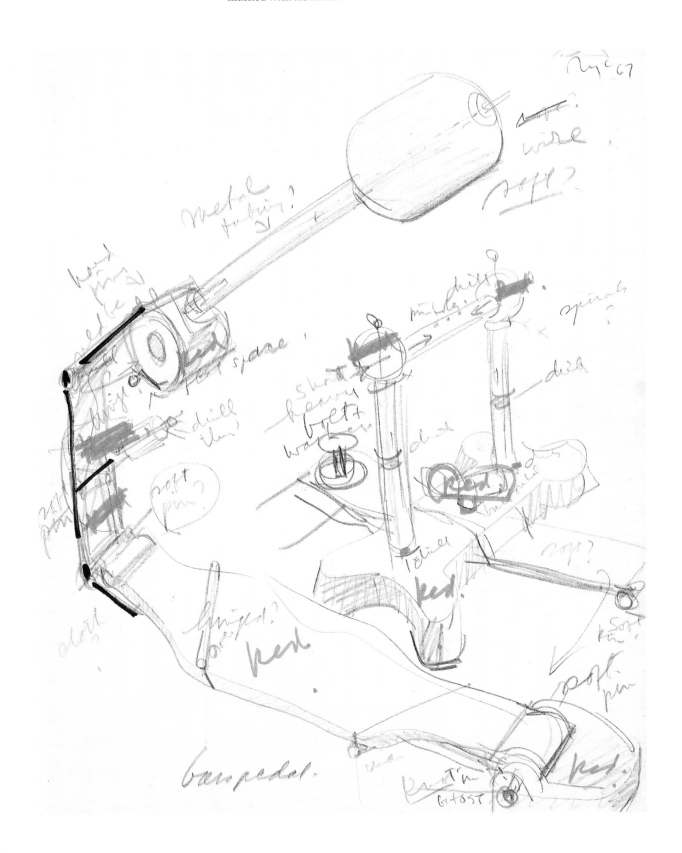

*Notebook Page: Metamorphic Studies
of Cartoon Mice, 'OHBOBOOY'*
Chicago, 1968
Pencil, coloured pencil, ball-point pen
Four notepages 2¾ × 5 in (6.3 × 12.7 cm)
on sheet 8⅝ × 6 in (22 × 15.2 cm)
on sheet 11 × 8½ in (28 × 21.6 cm)

The first attempts to include Mickey Mouse in the work were done in the fall of 1963 in a number of expressionistic variations, one of which became the poster for the first show in Los Angeles (Dwan Gallery, October 1963). Three years later, the result was more formalistic. By crossing Mickey Mouse with cameras and architecture, I arrived at the mechanical-looking version first known as *Strange Mickey Mouse* and later as the

Geometric Mouse. Along the way, in 1968, there were other hybridizations:
a.   An 'Oh Boy' balloon leaves the hand of a cartoon mouse with a 'hot dog' for a nose and 'his heart in his mouth'.
b.   A kite in the form of a Geometric Mouse head.
c.   Rear view of a Stuffed Animal Mouse with 'Stars in his Eyes'.
d.   Lollipop Mouse with 'Stars in his Eyes'.

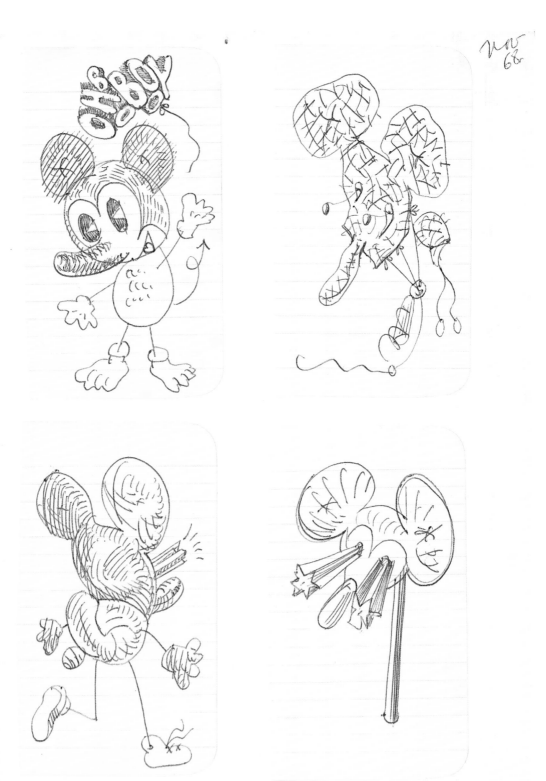

52

Notebook Page: Studies of the Mouse/Blimp
Los Angeles, 1968
pencil, coloured pencil, ball-point pen
sheets 2¾ × 5 in (6.3 × 12.7 cm)
in sheet 8⅝ × 6 in (21.3 × 15.2 cm)
in sheet 11 × 8½ in (28 × 21.6 cm)

The Mouse as a blimp, the result of frequent
sightings of the Goodyear Blimp, another Los
Angeles attraction. Top left: the Mouse/
Blimp approaching. Two motors (= eyes)
mounted on each side; steering is by the ears.
Nose = cabin. Below, Mouse/Blimp half
deflated in its hangar.

Notebook Page: Colossal Monument in the
Form of a Fire-plug, Navy Pier, Chicago
Los Angeles, 1968
Crayon, watercolour, pencil
on scrap 8¾ × 7 in (22.2 × 17.8 cm)
on sheet 11 × 8½ in (28 × 21.6 cm)

In 1968, for an emblem of the City of Chicago, I selected a characteristic type of fireplug found there, because of the city's identification with fire and water, and developed associations around it, civic and personal. This was before the first feasible

monument and the scale of the proposal is still fantastic. Navy Pier projects far into Lake Michigan and has been proposed for several colossal monuments, though only the fireplug is related in form to the domed hall with twin towers at the end of the pier.

Notebook Page: Flashlight Across the Hollywood Hills
February 1968
Pencil, ball-point pen
Sheets 5 × 8¼ in (12.8 × 21 cm)
and 3 × 8½ in (7.6 × 21.6 cm)
on sheet 11 × 8½ in (28 × 21.6 cm)

The first drawing of the flashlight subject. Its association with Hollywood probably is due to a recollection of the flashlights used by ushers to show patrons to their seats in movie theatres. In the Gemini edition of *Notes* (no. XII), which followed this drawing, the colossal flashlight became a dam: there actually is one above the city.

'The escaping water is coloured a hot yellow and is lighted at night . . . It gives all Hollywood the persistent sunset glow of far northern cities in summertime'. In a later drawing, the colossal flashlight was substituted for the Hoover Dam near Las Vegas.

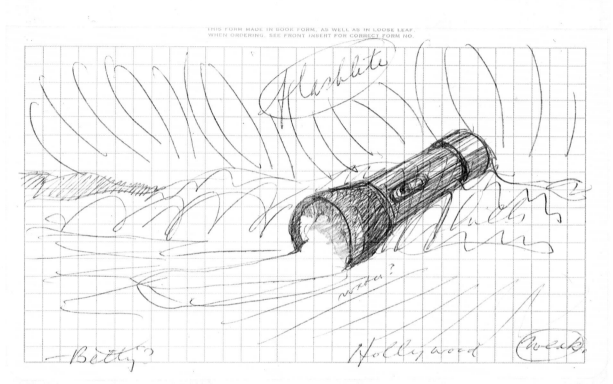

Notebook Page: Chocolate Earthquake
Los Angeles, 1968
Pencil, ball-point pen, clipping
11 × 8½ in (28 × 21.6 cm)

An advertisement in a Los Angeles paper,
suggesting a large scale through its closeup
view, evokes a comparison with the unstable
earth conditions of the area.

Notebook Page: Ionic Column/Fireplug
October 1968
Ball-point pen
Three sheets 5½ × 2¾ in (13.3 × 7 cm)
on sheet 11 × 8½ in (28 × 21.6 cm)

The combination of Chicago's classical
tradition with a contemporary functional
object recurs in the 100 foot *Batcolumn*
sculpture, erected there in 1977.

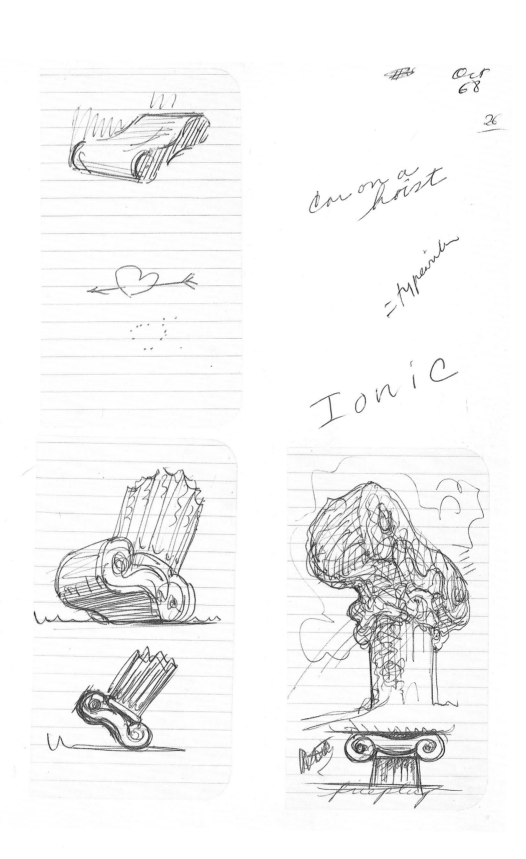

Notebook Page: Studies for the Giant Ice Bag
March–April 1969
Pencil, ball-point pen, felt pen
Sheets, odd sizes
on sheet 11 × 8½ in (28 × 21.6 cm)

At the time of this sketch, the material, mechanics and behaviour of the *Ice Bag* had not yet been determined. A comparison is made with the domes of the United States Capitol, which a month later results in the concept of a flexible, rotating Capitol Building. The sign of a head with an icebag, to signify hangover or headache, is always invoked by the press whenever the *Giant Ice Bag* is shown.

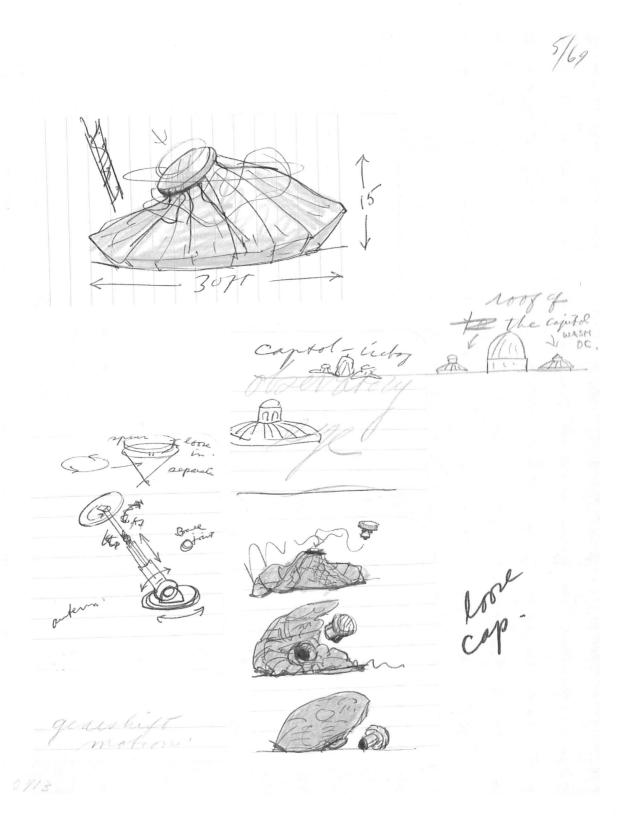

Notebook Page: Soft Rotating Capitol
April 1969
Crayon
Sheet 7¼ × 4½ in (18.4 × 11.4 cm)
on sheet 11 × 8½ in (28 × 21.6 cm)

The *Giant Ice Bag* was first exhibited in the United States Pavilion at the 1970 World's Fair in Osaka, where I discovered that icebags in Japan are more like a tube and are worn around the neck. Furthermore, the Japanese did not respond to the resemblance to Mt Fuji which seemed to me to make the Osaka site so appropriate.

Some spectators thought the *Ice Bag* was part of the space programme. There were several *Ice Bags* made afterwards but only one in the scale of the first one, which finally made it to Washington D.C. in 1985, in an exhibition of prints and projects by Gemini G.E.L. at the National Gallery.

Notebook Page: Fagend Canyon and
Burnt Bread Monument
December 1969
Ball-point pen, coloured pencil, pencil
Sheets, odd sizes
on sheet 11 × 8½ in (28 × 21.6 cm)

Two very ordinary artificial subjects become
involved with nature. The *Fagends* imitate
the pinnacles of Monument Valley, which
inspired George Herriman's Krazy Kat
landscapes. The *Bread Slice* becomes either a
cross-section of irregular rock or assumes the
profile of a cactus. A work is imagined
consisting of two 'slices', one like stainless
steel, the other rusted, or 'burnt'.

Notebook Page: Fagend Butte etc
December 1969
Ball-point pen, coloured pencil
Two sheets
on sheet 11 × 8½ in (28 × 21.6 cm)

The *Fagends* become chimney forms on a butte. These drawings are made in Los Angeles, where it is customary to cover oil derricks in urban areas, which then acquire a mysterious, monumental presence. The writing refers to streets in the city. La Brea is also the name given to the ancient tar pits behind the Los Angeles County Museum of Art. 'PINAKOTEXO' results spontaneously from the interplay of Pico Boulevard and Fairfax Avenue.

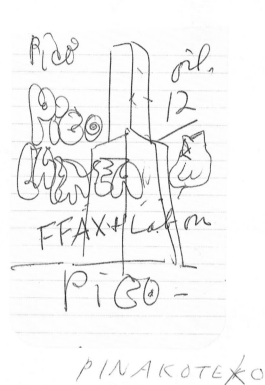

61

*Notebook Page: Building in the Form
of a Rack of Toast*
1970
Ball-point pen on clipping
4½ × 4½ in
(11.4 × 11.4 cm)
on sheet 11 × 8½ in (28 × 21.6 cm)

Toast, perfectly browned and sliced like a
roof, in a vaulted rack, make a structure
suitable to a modern cathedral. A fragment
of toast could serve as a sculpture at the
entrance.

London 4/70.

sculpture

" cathedral ?"

bldg.

Notebook Page: Costume
for a Drainpipe Ballet
Leningrad, 1970
Ball-point pen
Two sheets 4¾ × 4¾ in
(11.4 × 11.4 cm)
on sheet 11 × 8½ in
(28 × 21.6 cm)

On my only visit to Leningrad, in 1970, I was impressed by the large scale of drainpipes on its buildings and these became the leading subject of the place for me. Instead of a Colossal Monument, however, the *Drainpipe* in Russia might become the subject of an epic play, ballet or opera.

Notebook Page: Soft Inverted Windmill
1970
Ball-point pen
7¾ × 6 in (19.5 × 15.2 cm)

Cryptic reveries while flying reflect
experiences from my first visit to Holland.
A soft windmill crashes, teddybear-like,
perhaps dispatched by Don Quixote.
The windmill metamorphoses into a soft
baseball bat, which splits, revealing a
soft alphabet.

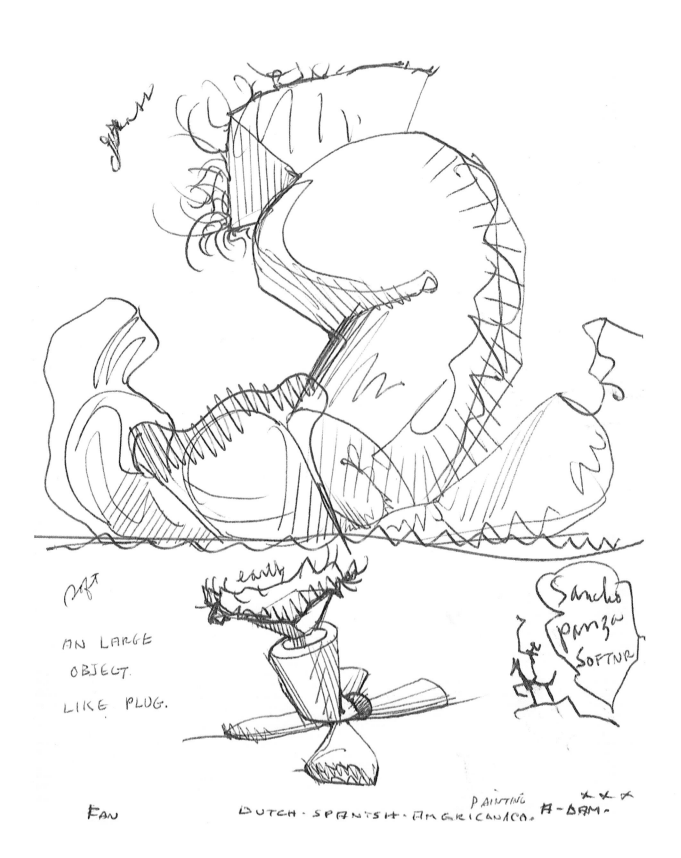

AN LARGE
OBJECT.
LIKE PLUG.

Sancho
panza
SOFTNR

FAN

DUTCH · SPANISH · AMERICANICA.

PAINTING
A-ARM.

Notebook Page: Soft, Split Bat/Alphabet
1970
Ball-point pen
7¾ × 6 in (19.5 × 15.2 cm)

Notebook Page: Beach House in the Form of Melting Butter
1972
Ball-point pen, watercolour
Sheet 5⅛ × 2¾ in (13 × 7 cm)
on sheet 11 × 8½ in (28 × 21.6 cm)

After a visit to Lake Sunapee in New Hampshire in 1971, I made several studies for a summer house in the shape of food flowing or dripping off the steep shores of the lake. The food chosen had to have an architectural character; besides the butter I proposed a design based on a slice of blueberry pie.

butter beach house

Notebook Page: Baked Potato, with Butter,
in Place of Alcatraz Island
1972
Ball-point pen and coloured pencil
Two sheets 5½ × 2¾ in (14 × 7 cm)
on sheet 11 × 8½ in (28 × 21.6 cm)

The melting butter pat is equated with the
setting sun, sinking behind a landscape of the
Baked Potato, before the Golden Gate in San
Francisco. This is one of several responses to
published discussions about redesigning the
former island prison.

Notebook Page: Knäckebröd Q
1974
Pencil, ball-point pen
Three sheets
on sheet 11 × 8½ in (28 × 21.6 cm)

The *Inverted Q* sculpture was developed as a commission for Akron, Ohio, to be executed by one of its rubber factories. It was to be pneumatic, like a tyre, but anti-functional, incapable of turning, hence the horn or tail which makes it a Q. The Q is here seen as a fragment of the body around the navel, which is compared to a fragment of Knäckebröd, leading to another sculpture, in metal or ceramic. The heart, cherry with stem, and question-mark are forms related to the *Inverted Q*, the final via the first letter of the word 'question' as well as its shape. Blood might accompany the isolation of an actual body fragment, but not in art. A section of heart with vein is drawn as a primitive 'iron'.

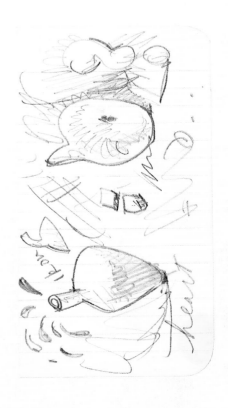

Notebook Page: Button Studies
1975
Pencil, ball-point pen
Four sheets
on sheet 11 × 8½ in (28 × 21.6 cm)

The button subject, considered for sites in Los Angeles. A button house on the edge of a cliff is produced by extending the holes into solid columns. The drawing of this is given a 'F.L.W.' (Frank Lloyd Wright) perspective, from below, as in certain renderings of his houses for the San Francisco area.

A tilted concrete button sculpture is thought of for the sculpture garden at the University of California. Lower left, a grand piano without its legs, stuck into the ground, 'equals' a bicycle seat; below that, a harp in its box.

Notebook Page: Cocktail Sign
Comparisons
1979
Pencil, ball-point pen
Three sheets
on sheet 11 × 8½ in (28 × 21.6 cm)

Taverns, in San Francisco particularly, announce themselves by a simple neon sign showing a cocktail glass with a cherry or an olive on a toothpick. While developing a sculpture on this subject, I noted the presence of this basic scheme in the representation of other subjects, in a more or less far-fetched way.

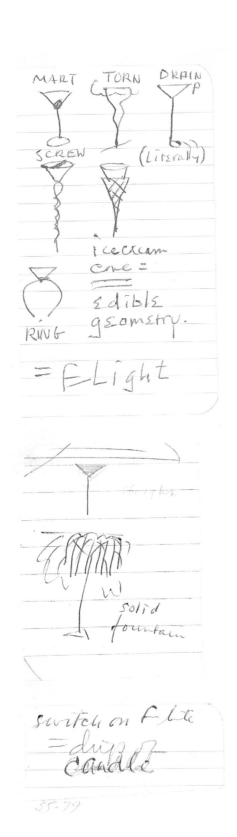

*Notebook Page: Tilting Cocktail
in the Vitra Factory Site*
1983
Pencil, felt pen
11 × 8½ in (28 × 21.6 cm)

The cocktail, tilted as if drunk, was an
unrealized early proposal for the Vitra
Factory, in Weil-am-Rhein, site of the
Balancing Tools. The sculpture was intended
as a birthday present for the founder of the
factory from his son; hence the emphasis on
celebration. The factory makes chairs of
stainless steel; it is imagined that the
chromium covered tubing of a steel chair
has been reformed into the cocktail.

Notebook Page: Bread Slices and Nails
1979
Pencil
Two sheets
on sheet 11 × 8½ in (28 × 21.6 cm)

An exhibition of thin slices: Dutch
pumpernickel to Melba Toast. Below, eroded
nails at the edge of existence.
Each time the pioneers in America moved on,
they burnt their wooden houses to recover
the precious nails.

6/79

*Notebook Page: Sliced Berries
and Squashed Butt*
1981
Pencil and coloured pencil
Sheet 5⅛ × 2¾ in (13 × 7 cm)
on sheet 11 × 8½ in (28 × 21.6 cm)

Little pieces of flotsam demand recording.
These turned up during a dinner in Cologne.

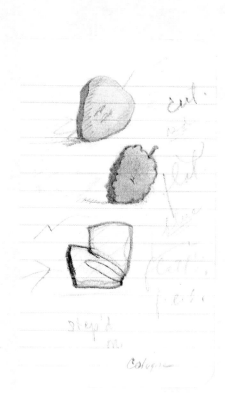

Notebook Page: Studies of Tumbling and Rolling Hats in a Field for Salinas, California
February 1980
Pencil
Three sheets:
two 2¾ × 5 in (7 × 12.7 cm);
one 4¼ × 8½ in (10.8 × 21 cm)
on sheet 11 × 8½ in (28 × 21.6 cm)

The site in Salinas, California, was an open field adjacent to the rodeo stand. Coosje suggested a hat rolling across the field. We eventually decided on a hat sailing down, in three stages of landing.

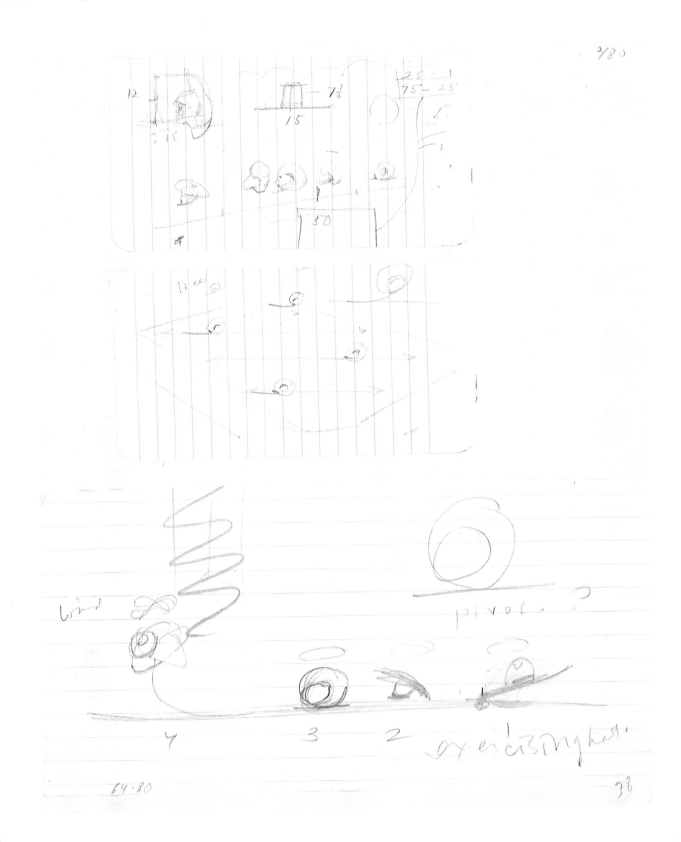

Notebook Page: Thumb-tack Through
Paper, Nails Through Wood
1982
Felt pen
Sheet 5⅛ × 8½ in (13 × 21 cm)
on sheet 11 × 8½ in (28 × 21.6 cm)

There are some subjects which hang around
but never seem to get anywhere. Among these
are the thumb-tack and the nail, less
interesting than their cousin, the devious
Screw. There is little a nail or tack can do but
push its way through something, but I
continue to try them in different situations.

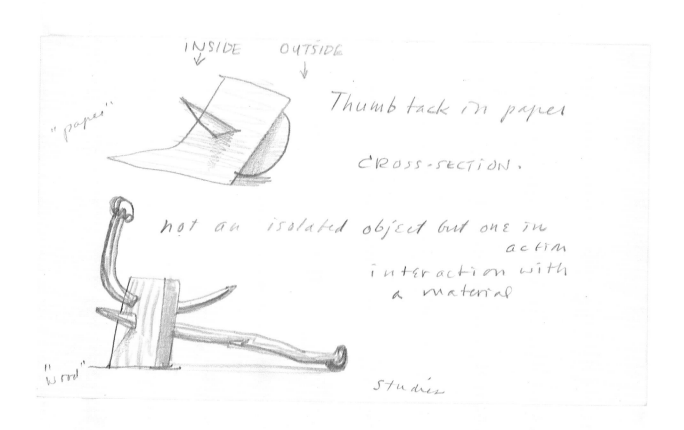

INSIDE   OUTSIDE

"paper"

Thumb tack in paper

CROSS-SECTION.

not an isolated object but one in
action
interaction with
a material

"wood"

studies

82-82

Notebook Page: Giant 'Jacks' Objects
Made of Tools
May 1983
Pencil, watercolour
Sheet 5⅛ × 8½ in (13 × 21 cm)
on sheet 11 × 8½ in (28 × 21.6 cm)

A proposal for a large outdoor sculpture
using tools combined like an object in a game
of 'jacks'. Each arm can be a different tool or
three different tools can intersect. Later, the
pliers, hammer and screwdriver were
combined to form a gate, which led to the
sculpture of the *Balancing Tools*.

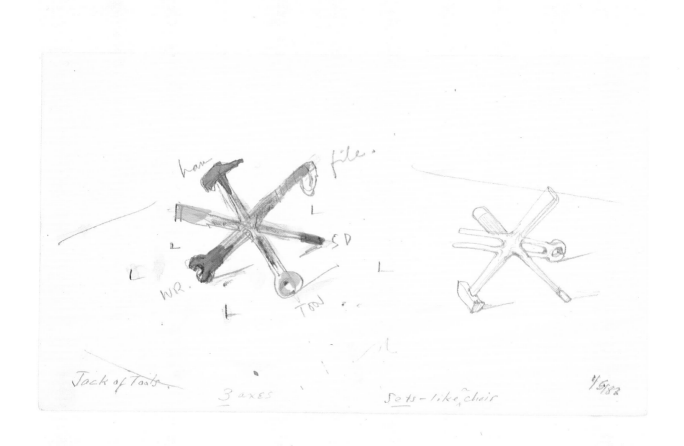

Notebook Page: Knäckebröd/Iron
1986
Felt pen, photocopy
11 × 8½ in (28 × 21.6 cm)

Eating Knäckebröd is like eating wood, metal or stone, and it is adaptable to many subjects. Here, a fragment of Knäckebröd resembling the profile of an iron also suggests a seashore cliff, such as those painted by Courbet or Monet. The image was first drawn on a napkin, then reproduced by xerox and coloured.

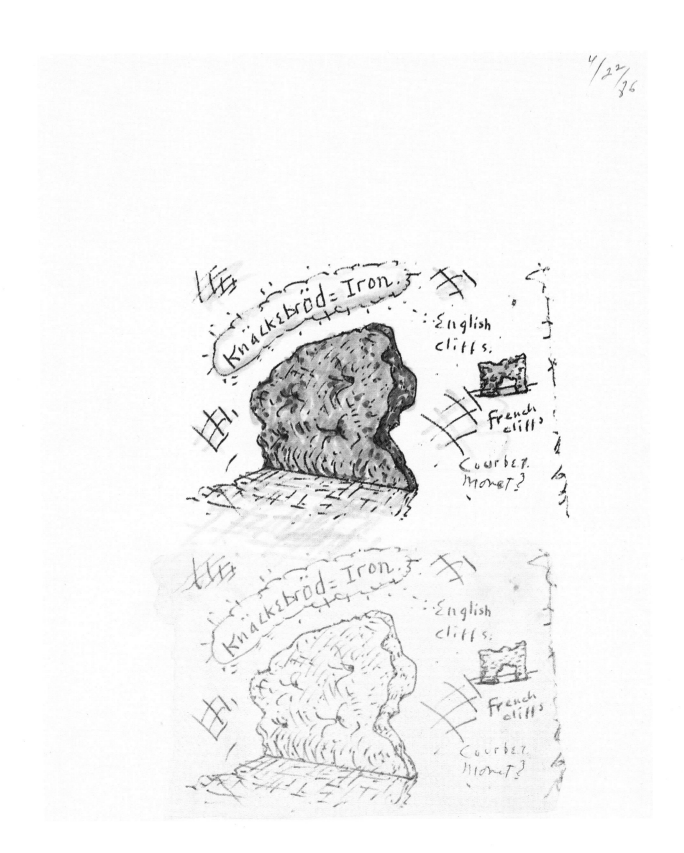

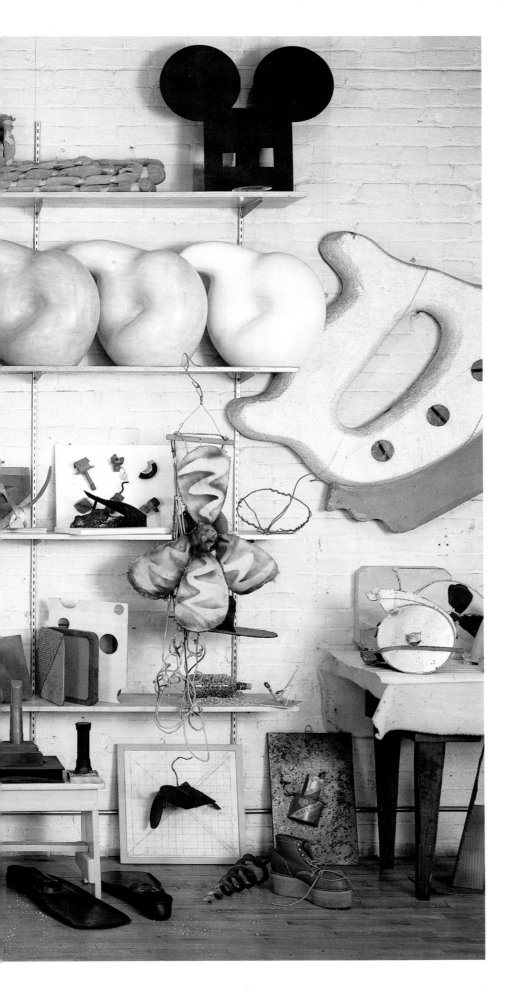

Models

Baked Potato Multiple, Painted Prototype
1965
Cast resin, acrylic, on porcelain plate
8½ × 4¾ × 5¼ in (21.6 × 12 × 13.3 cm)
Edition of 75

Stylized food, like an ice cream cone or
a baked potato, is somewhat unpredictable
but always within certain limits. What counts
is the creation of a double identity for the
work as both pure thing and art. A base for
example is equated with a plate. This model
served as a guide to the paint strokes on the
seventy-five copies in the edition. Afterwards
I put the finishing touch on each by spraying
green paint (= chives), using a toothbrush.

Circular Saw Model
1964
Cardboard, paper, tape
spray enamel
10 × 10½ × 13½ in
(25.4 × 26.7 × 34.3 cm)

A sophisticated piece of machinery
impressionistically sketched in simple
materials found around the studio
in Venice, California.

Study for a Sculpture in the Form
of an Outboard Motor
1965
Clay over object, metal, wood
8½ × 6⅜ × 3½ in (21 × 16.2 × 8.9 cm)

A toy is often taken as the starting point of a sculpture based on an object, because it has already undergone simplification in the direction of a stereotype. By the application of clay, the object is carried towards organic form, the reverse of what happens to the bone which turns into a spaceship in the prelude to the film '2001'. The steering stick begins to resemble a branch.

Study for Hanging Soft Fan
1966
Canvas, cord, wood, cardboard
spray enamel
45 × 13 × 11 in
(114.3 × 33 × 27.9 cm)

One of the first attempts to 'soften' a fan by substituting canvas and cord for metal and wire. The subject was an old-fashioned fan, probably from the late 1920s , which seemed to typify the object more than later streamlined versions. The experiments culminated in 1967 in the *Giant Soft Fan*, in vinyl, and the *Giant Soft Fan, Ghost Version*, in canvas, now respectively in the Museum of Modern Art, New York and Houston Museum of Fine Arts.

Miniature Soft Drum Set
1967
Canvas, washline, wood
on cardboard base; spray enamel
10 × 19 × 14 in
(25.4 × 48.3 × 35.6 cm)

The drum set, in its many parts, with its hard
and stretched surfaces reduced to cloth,
becomes a mountain landscape, endlessly
rearrangeable. Larger versions were done
afterwards in vinyl and canvas as well as a
more artificial multiple edition.

English Light Switch
1966
Plaster, metal, tempera
1¾ × 5⅛ × 6 in
(4.4 × 13 × 15.2 cm)

The interest in light switches, begun in Los Angeles in 1963, carried over to England three years later. British switches were different and there were many kinds. My plan was to identify three or four typical ones, do my versions, and cast them, attaching a magnet in back so that they could be stuck to and moved about on a piece of metal covered with typical British wallpaper. This project was never completed, but some of the originals remain, of which this is one. It is painted to suggest the wallpaper on which it might be mounted.

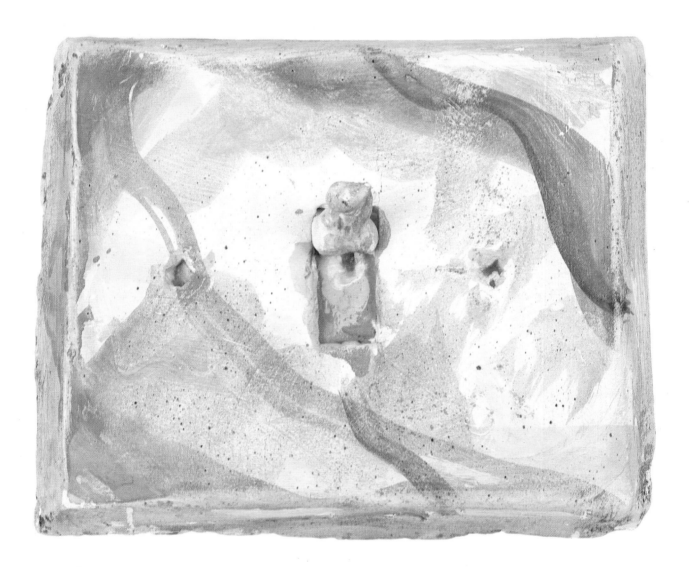

Fireplug Multiple, Trial Proof
1968
Plaster, acrylic
8 × 8 × 6 in (20.3 × 20.3 × 15.2 cm)
Edition of 100

The emblem of Chicago became a souvenir of the events and demonstrations surrounding the Democratic Convention in August 1968. Notes from that time describe the project: 'Should be made of cheap plaster, painted red and glossy and be like a breakable prize one wins at an amusement park for knocking down a pyramid of soft bottles.

One plug should be set aside to be thrown through the plate glass of the gallery window, to launch the protest exhibition.'
The exhibition referred to was held at the Feigen Gallery in October 1968 to raise money for a legal defense fund to assist persons arrested in the demonstrations.

Monument for Yale University: Giant Traveling and Telescoping Lipstick with Changeable Parts Showing Three Stages of Extension, Presentation Model
1969
Cardboard, canvas, painted and shellacked
Tractor: 5½ × 16½ × 29½ in
(14 × 42 × 65 cm)
Lipstick, stage one: 4 × 8½ × 10¼ in
(10.2 × 21.7 × 26 cm) stage two: 14½ × 8½
× 10¼ in (36.8 × 21.7 × 26 cm) stage three:
23½ × 8½ × 10¼ in (59.7 × 21.7 × 26 cm)

The *Lipstick Ascending on Caterpillar Tracks* was first conceived as a remote-controlled, motorised work that would crawl into position on the campus site and thereafter serve as a platform for student speeches. When someone wanted to speak, they would mount the *Lipstick* deck and pump up the stick to get attention. After the speech, the stick would sink down. Three stages are shown which can be substituted on the carriage. Later, the motor was eliminated and the lipstick sculpture was carried in parts to the site for assembly. A soft lipstick was inflated at the installation but it did not rise and fall. Afterwards a rigid lipstick made of plastic was permanently substituted for the soft one.

87

Fragment of an Ionic Column
1968
Cardboard, spray enamel
9½ × 9 × 6¼ in
(24.1 × 22.9 × 15.9 cm)

Originally a counterpart to a cardboard version of the Chicago *Fireplug*, this was later seen as a possible design for a house in the ruin folly style, for someplace in the American South.

Fagend Study
1968
Plaster, canvas, acrylic
10½ × 5½ × 3¼ in
(26.7 × 14 × 8.3 cm)

A fagend is an object showing the result of a destructive process. In making a *Fagend* sculpture, the object is first recreated in a larger scale, easy in this case because it's just a soft cylinder, more or less filled; then the effect of a stubbed out butt is re-staged in a controlled, ideal way.

Fagends come in all sizes, materials and moods; this one is rigid and thickly painted as one would paint and repaint ventilators on a ship, which tends to undercut the pathos.

Chocolate Earthquake Segment
1969
Cardboard, canvas, wood, acrylic
15 × 12 × 7 in (38 × 31 × 18 cm)

As part of the Art and Technology programme of the Los Angeles County Museum, I spent two weeks at the Walt Disney factory observing the manufacture of robots and illusions for Disneyland. A mechanical earthquake in the form of a crumbling chocolate bar was one of the results.

Icebag II, Model
1969
Cardboard, painted cloth, wood
10 × 16 × 4 in (50.8 × 40.6 × 11.4 cm)

Early in 1969, the *Ice Bag* was one of the unrealized proposals for Oberlin College, where the *Three-Way Plug* was eventually sited in 1970. But the climate of Ohio was not suited to such a vulnerable, sensuous construction. The *Ice Bag* fared better when transplanted to Southern California, later in the year. This sketch was done at Walt Disney's in Burbank, but when Disney later withdrew from the Art and Technology programme the *Bag* was completed by Gemini G.E.L., in Los Angeles.

Proposal for a Catalog of My Retrospective
Exhibition in the Form of a Swiss
Cheese Sandwich
1969
Cardboard, spray, enamel
14½ × 12¾ × 3¼ in (36.8 × 32.4 × 8.3 cm)

The text is divided into two equal shapes of
bound pages; square, with rounded corners,
the 'bread slices'. Between them is a loose
'slice of Swiss cheese' made of plastic,
like a book mark. The three elements are held
together but not attached in a cover of
corrugated cardboard. An attempt to equate
the form of the book with its contents.

Geometric Mouse, Original Model
1969
Cardboard, metal, string, wood
10⅜ × 6½ × 10 in (26.3 × 15.9 × 25.4 cm)
on base ½ × 15¼ × 15¾ in
1.3 × 38.7 × 25.4 cm)

The *Geometric Mouse* image, flat as a cinema plane, was converted to a sculpture by bending the appendages into a tripod stance. The eyes were opened like hatches, and chains which drooped to the ground, ending in discs, were attached to them (= tear or shade-pull). The *Geometric Mouse* became a multiple in five different scales, each defined by the diameter of its ears. There is only one

of the largest, with a nine foot ear, now in Houston, Texas. Of the 2 foot, there are twenty four; of the 9 inch, one hundred. The 6 inch one, which is close to the scale of the original model and also made of paper, though white and adjustable, is an unlimited edition. There was to be a *Geometric Mouse* for every situation, indoor/outdoor, private/public, or rich/poor.

Saw Handle Model
1968
Expanded polystyrene, cardboard
43½ × 58 × 5 in
(110.5 × 147.3 × 12.7 cm)

The *Giant Saw* was commissioned by the Vancouver Art Gallery and executed in the city after the model. In the finished work the wooden handle hangs against the wall while the aluminium blade, hinged at two breaks, droops onto the floor in a denial of its function.

Later, several models of a much larger, rigid version cutting across a plaza were made, as a large scale proposal for a World's Fair held in Spokane, Washington, in 1974.

Study for a Sculpture in the Form
of a Saw Cutting
1973
Cardboard, spray enamel
14⅛ × 10 × 10 in (36 × 25.4 × 25.4 cm)

*Study for a Civic Sculpture in the Form
of a Mitt and Ball*
1972
Object painted with acrylic, metal, wood
9⅞ × 10 × 12¼ in (25 × 25.4 × 31 cm)

The *Standing Mitt with Ball* was proposed
for my first urban commission in 1972, a
matching grant for downtown Lansing,
Michigan. The proposal was turned
down but the subject was later realized in a
12 foot high lead and steel version which now
stands at Wave Hill Park in the Bronx,
New York City.

The model is made from a miniature toy set
of Mitt, Ball and Bat bought in a Woolwort
store (Mouse Museum No. 262). A tracing
the toy mitt was the starting point of the
larger version.

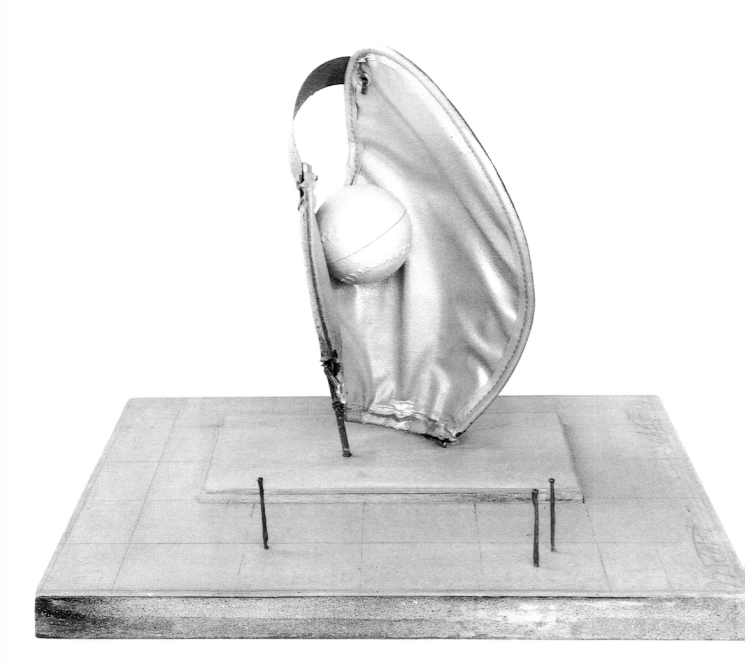

Inverted Q
1974
Ceramic, painted
5¼ × 5¼ × 4⅜ in
(13.3 × 13.3 × 11.1 cm)

The *Inverted Q* was put through the stages of development of a tyre, from carving in plaster to molding in an oven. The history of the *Inverted Q* also included a ceramic edition by Helena Uglow which had the surface of a fresh galosh, of which this is a trial proof.

The final version, at 6 feet, for which a large enough oven could not be found, was done as a casting in concrete instead. At Coosje's suggestion, it was painted pink, like the rubber balls she had observed children playing with in the streets of New York City.

Study for the 'Wayside Drainpipe'
1978
Chalk, wood, cardboard, spray enamel
11 × 9⅜ × 5⅝ in (28 × 23.8 × 14 cm)

The *Drainpipe* subject originated in an advertisement in a Stockholm newspaper in 1966. Because of its association with the letter T, it was later developed into a Colossal Monument Proposal for Toronto, with a swimming pool on top, for the site now occupied by the Canadian Pacific Tower. Its signification of a link between sky and earth, and its resemblance to a cross produced the *Wayside Drainpipe* sculpture, sited near Münster in 1979.

Preliminary Model for the Crusoe Umbrella
1978
Coated wire
9¹³/₁₆ × 14½ in (25 × 37 cm)

One of several preliminary studies for the
large-scale *Crusoe Umbrella* in Des Moines,
Iowa, completed in 1979.
From the beginning, the subject was equated
with plants. This study is tendril-like;
another was made from a defoliated
Christmas tree.

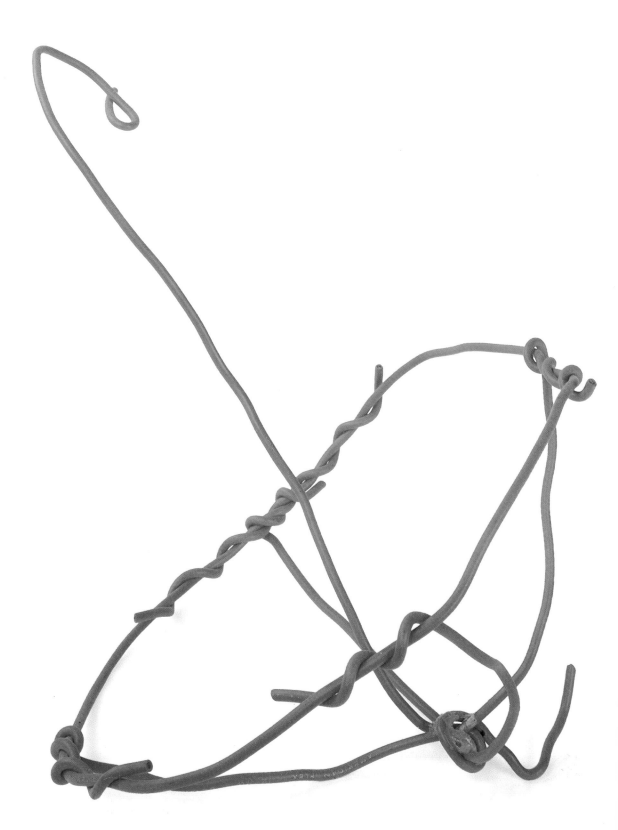

Flashlight
1979
Object in plaster, painted
$7^{5}/_{8} \times 4 \times 4^{7}/_{8}$ in
$(19.4 \times 10.2 \times 12.4$ cm$)$

Flashlight, Study
1979
Paper, wood, painted
11½ × 6⅛ × 5¾ in
(29.2 × 15.6 × 14.6 cm)

The *Flashlight*, installed at the University of
Nevada at Las Vegas in 1981, began with an
ordinary flashlight of this particular kind
which was later transformed by arranging
profiles taken from it around a cylinder, all
painted black. In the daytime the shadows
made by the profiles create the effect of a
densely black object, a piece of darkness left
over from the night. At night, the sculpture is
nearly invisible; its only light is a glow
around the base simulating the effect of a
flashlight standing on its face.

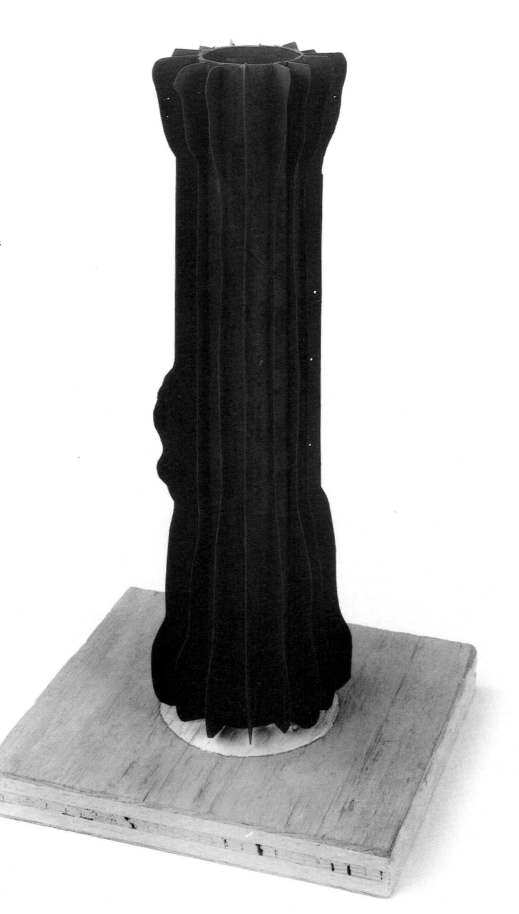

Study for Salinas Hat
1980
Grinding wheel, plastic cup, sand, acrylic
7 × 5 × 4½ in (17.8 × 12.7 × 11.4 cm)

The first model of the hat, which was to be more in the direction of a field-worker's hat than that of a cowboy, was improvised from a plastic cup combined with a grinding wheel, commonplace objects in the Lippincott factory.

The hat was coated with glue and rolled in the sand of the yard. Three of them, mounted in a row at different heights, served to present our idea of the *Hat in Three Stages of Landing* to the committee in Salinas.

*Study for a Sculpture in the Form
of a Split Button*
1981
Cardboard, enamel
7¾ × 11½ × 10½ in
(19.7 × 29.2 × 26.7 cm)

Coosje choose the button for a sculpture to lie on the ground in front of the Library at the University of Pennsylvania in Philadelphia, but suggested breaking it to disrupt its symmetry. In the course of cutting a cardboard model in half, the possibilities

of just bending the button were discovered. Coosje later pushed the peak down, making a more precarious equilibrium which formed two gentle slopes on which the students could sit.

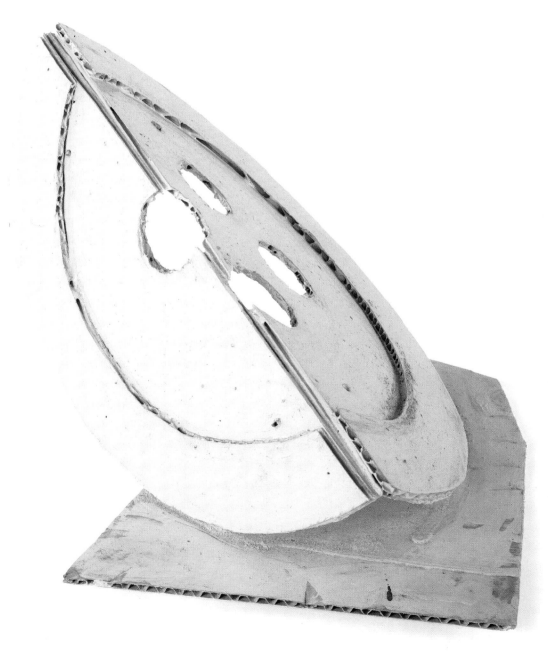

Souvenir of Documenta 7
Beschmierte Friderick
1982
Plaster, enamel
$7\frac{5}{8} \times 3\frac{1}{8} \times 3\frac{1}{8}$ in
$(19.4 \times 7.9 \times 7.9$ cm$)$

The statue of Frederick II of Hessen stands on a pedestal in front of the Fridericianum in Kassel. During Documenta 7, I thought of coating the statue with silicone, or something which could later be peeled off, and painting graffiti over it, imitating what has been done to the statue of George Washington at the Brooklyn end of the Williamsburgh Bridge. But instead, I did an edition of a small version of the sculpture, hand-painted in a graffiti style, which was sold at the Fashion MODA concession in the park. The form is cursory and soupy in order to merge with the strokes of paint.

Altered Souvenir of the Cologne Cathedral
1980
Metal, plaster, enamel
7½ × 6½ × 3½ in (19 × 16.5 × 8.8 cm)

In response to a commission to a number of artists to create works commemorating the centennial of the completion of the Cologne cathedral, I bought a pot-metal souvenir, coated it with plaster and then recast it, thus reducing the authoritarian edifice to the comforting appearance of a small animal. My intention was to create a parallel line of souvenirs, but the project was never fully carried out. One casting, painted silver, was included in the reconstruction of *The Store* for the exhibition 'Westkunst' in Cologne in 1981, and presented to the 100,000th visitor to the exhibition.

Tilting Neon Cocktail, Study
1983
Wood, cardboard, painted
17^{15}/$_{16}$ × 9^{1}/$_{4}$ × 11^{9}/$_{16}$ in
(45.5 × 23.5 × 29.5 cm)

Tilting Neon Cocktail, Multiple
1983
Stainless steel, aluminium, acrylic
on plexiglass base
18⅜ × 7 × 6¼ in (46.7 × 17.8 × 15.9 cm)
Edition of 50

The cocktail glass eventually became a
multiple made to benefit The New Museum
of Contemporary Art in New York City.
The source of the subject is not the cocktail
itself but the sign version of it, in neon tubing.
There can be no interruption in neon tubing;
this requirement is applied to the work,
which is made of a single rod of highly
polished stainless steel. The two dimensional
sign is projected into three dimensions,
creating an illusion of the absent glass and
liquid. This abstraction is contrasted with the
realistically rendered olive and toothpick,
given a painterly treatment to set it off from
the slick production of the rest. In the final
version, the *Neon Cocktail* is tilting on the
fragment of a black plexiglass table, like a
dancer in a 1930s musical. I visualized a long
table for the donors elegantly set with all
fifty cocktails.

Balancing Tools, Model
1983
Cardboard, metal, wood, painted
11⁷/₁₆ × 9⁷/₁₆ × 14½ in
(29 × 24 × 37 cm)

Since the Vitra factory, in front of which the sculpture was to stand, is located in the countryside, Coosje had the idea of an industrialized garden gate, leading into the orchard in front of the offices. The impossible equilibrium, easy to arrange in the nearly weightless cardboard model, was fortunately preserved in the steel version 26 feet high. The tools are dancing like the Griffon, Lion and the Wildman of Basel folklore in their Rite of Spring.

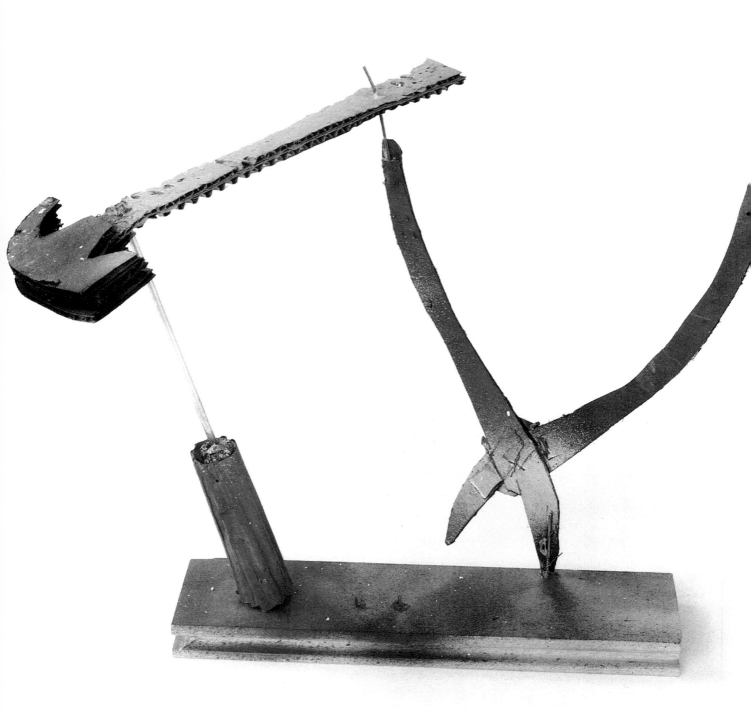

Toppling Ladder with Spilling Paint,
Fabrication Model
1986
Steel, enamel
18⅜ × 12 × 12 in
(46.7 × 30.5 × 30.5 cm)

The *Toppling Ladder* is a sculpture made
specifically for the architectural landscape
created by the architect Frank O. Gehry at
the Loyola Law School in downtown Los
Angeles. An enlarged version of chain-link
fencing is substituted for the ladder's
steps and braces as a kind of homage to
this most humble building material often
used by Gehry.

Three-Way Plug

Facing page:
Floating Three-Way Plug
1976
Colour etching
49¼ × 38¼ in (125 × 97.2 cm)
Printed at Crown Point Press
Oakland, California
Published by Multiples, Inc
New York

Log of the Three-Way Plug

Claes Oldenburg

The concern with electrical subjects, begun in 1963 in Los Angeles, continued in 1965 in the new studio in New York with, among others, the *Fan* and the *Three-Way Plug*. The first *Three-Way Plug* was built of cardboard, following the usual approach of establishing my version of the object suitable for translation into different materials. In 1968, the cardboard *Plug* was destroyed when a workman at Documenta 4 fell on it. In the course of reconstructing it, I made one that was twice as large, in masonite and plywood. This became the prototype for the more refined versions, in mahogany and cherrywood, which looked like 1930s radio sets. Patterns made from these became blueprints for the steel and bronze versions. Along the way, as with all the electrical objects, there were parallel soft versions, in canvas, denim, vinyl and leather using the patterns of the hard ones. The *Three-Way Plug* was especially suitable for pattern-making. The use of fabric to make objects began in the environments and 'theatre of objects' in 1961–62. The transformation makes the object more subject to circumstances, especially gravity, makes it go with forces rather than strain against them, and it makes the object totally unfunctional. Add to this the symbolism of a slack, floppy condition (but this comes after the wish to see the effect of the transformation just for itself), the comedy of rendering the object useless and into another, unpredictable dimension.

From 1963 on I was deliberately taking a subject and running it through different scales, materials and functions by means of simultaneous identifications: paper = steel = cloth; plug = building = balloon. And identification of opposites: large = small, distant = close, many = one. I didn't think so much of the resulting content, whether a plug made of cloth expressed 'dissolution'. I was behaving more like an inventor, trying different possibilities, like the description I read of Edison trying to solve the problem of the light bulb, except that each discovery was an end in itself. The scale and complexity of the experiments kept increasing as my access to different kinds of fabrication widened. Carpentry and upholstery were added to sewing; then steel manufacturing, mechanical engineering and architecture. Softening is not melting or dissolving, it is altering the walls. The seams are still there. It is another kind of architecture. It is a way to reduce a banal form, any form, to zero from which one can make anything one wants out of it, including art. A softened form has something of the free potential of drawing. The *Three-Way Plug* was always considered as a floating object, either in water or air, or as an object dropped from the sky or more or less deflated, like a balloon. This was a stratagem to avoid a base, in one way or another; to give the object independence. In the floating versions, I can't suspend gravity, much as I'd like to, so they are always hanging. Another characteristic of the presentation of the subject is the concealment of a third or half of it; its presence in two states of matter, air/water, air/earth. The *Three-Way Plug* is good for this approach because of its symmetrical construction; as with the earth, one always knows the shape of the other or hidden side. The architectural character and potential of the *Plug* became apparent the moment it was imagined in colossal form, as in the *Floating Plug*. Because of its crossed vaults it suggested a cathedral, having even a sort of resemblance to the Hagia Sophia. This way of seeing the plug, which is a sculpture with an interior and with windows, led to a series of building proposals in the form of plugs, including the variations of the subject discovered in Sweden and England in 1966.

Colossal Floating Three-Way Plug
1965
Pencil on paper
30 × 22 in (76.2 × 55.9 cm)
Walker Art Center, Minneapolis

Notebook Page: Three-Way Plug Studies
Dallas 1970
Ball-point pen, coloured pencil
Four sheets 5 × 2¾ in (12.6 × 7 cm)
on sheet 11 × 8½ in (28 × 21.6 cm)

An elongated *Three-Way Plug* was tried as a variant of windmill architecture, as an example of the larger scale I was seeking in object-sculpture. The large soft version of the *Three-Way Plug* planned for a home site in Dallas was eventually realized in the scale of the steel and bronze version at 12 feet, in two colours of vinyl, one for the Des Moines Art Center (blue, 1971) and the other for the Walker Art Center (brown, 1975). Art with insides which has apertures may be described as 'eyes' art; for example, the *Geometric Mouse*. Or in the case of the *Three-Way Plug* one might speak of 'nostril art', making a comparison with Donald Duck's bill.

Giant Three-Way Plug, Scale B, 3/3
1970
Cherrywood
58½ × 39 × 28½ in
(148.6 × 99 × 72.4 cm)
Philadelphia Museum of Art
Philadelphia, Pennsylvania

Three-Way Plug, Scale B, Soft
1970
Leather, wood
72 × 36 × 11 in
(182.9 × 91.4 × 27.9 cm)
Collection William J. Hokin
Chicago

Three-Way Plug
1966
Cardboard, painted
and shellacked
39⅜ × 25³⁄₁₆ × 19¼ in
(100 × 64 × 49 cm)
Collection Hubert Peeters
Linkebeek, Belgium

The Broome Street studio in 1971, showing, left to right: one of the *Geometric Mouse Banners*, stretched from the ceiling; template for *Lipstick for Marilyn Monroe*, 1967, inverted, on wall; *Saw Handle Model*, leaning against a template for the rear end of the *Airflow*, 1966; pattern for *Mug*, a sculpture from *The Street*, 1960; *Denim Plug*, suspended over patterns including the *Screw*, a smaller version of the *Plug* in canvas and a photostat of the *Swedish Extension Plug*. Far right, an aluminium version of the *Trowel* and another pattern for the *Airflow*.

Giant Three-Way Plug, Scale A, 1/3
1970
Cor-Ten steel and bronze
116^{15}/$_{16}$ × 77^{1}/$_{8}$ × 57^{13}/$_{16}$ in
(297 × 196 × 147 cm)
Situated beside the Allen Memorial Art
Museum, Oberlin, Ohio

Three-Way Plug, Position Studies
1970
Six objects in painted plaster
4^{3}/$_{4}$ × 4^{3}/$_{4}$ × 4^{3}/$_{4}$ in (12 × 12 × 12 cm each)
Collection Mr and Mrs Parks Campbell
Fort Worth, Texas

Some Observations on Oldenburg's Alternative Proposal for an Addition to the Allen Memorial Art Museum, Oberlin, Ohio

Coosje van Bruggen

In 1970 the *Giant 3-Way Plug* was placed on the sloping lawn beside the Allen Memorial Art Museum, which was designed by Cass Gilbert and built from 1915 to 1917 in a Tuscan Renaissance style with Romanesque elements. In choosing this site Oldenburg related the structural elements of the *Plug* to the architecture of the Museum building.

In her article on the *Giant 3-Way Plug* Ellen Johnson observed that: 'The *Plug* matches the Renaissance design in its combination of rectilinear and curvilinear elements and in its strict bilateral symmetry, which is, however, hidden, almost denied, by its partly submerged, dropped position.'[1] Oldenburg used a plug purchased in an Oberlin hardware store to position the sculpture. Half buried, on a diagonal axis with its prongs upward, the *Plug* appears more as a sculpture than an architectural structure, which in this position would be in some sort of distress. The aggressive diagonal extends into space, increasing the effect of the sculpture in relation to the mass of the building.

Another consideration in placing the *Plug* beside the Museum was to strongly contrast its banal, contemporary context, due to its mass-production origin, with the glorification of the past that the Museum's design suggests. Oldenburg knew at the time that the *Giant 3-Way Plug* would have to make way for the construction of a new wing. Early in 1975 the *Plug* was removed and placed in outdoor storage, and construction began on the addition which had been designed by Venturi and Rauch in 1974.

Venturi, writing about the project, discussed the juxtaposition of classical style and contemporary banality he found in Oberlin, a typical Midwestern town: 'The Art Museum achieves harmony through contrast, heightening the quality of its context through jarring juxtapositions such as terra-cotta friezes with moulded plastic signs; della Robbia tondos with Citgo logos; decorative wrought-iron grilles with ginger-bread wooden trellises; pilasters and urns with gas pumps and signs; and a front porch completing a classical axis. Diverse elements give context for, and enhance each other, like Pop Art beer cans in a white-walled gallery. One Allen Memorial Art Museum does not a Fiesole make; on the contrary, it makes Oberlin more what it is.'[2] This observation recalls Oldenburg's intention in placing a sculpture in the form of a common object next to the Museum building.

Venturi's analysis of how the pop elements in the environment and the Museum enhance one another through contrast does not seem to have contributed much to his design of the new wing. He arrived at a solution not out of aesthetic preference as Oldenburg was free to do in his sculpture, but through the practical aims of the building programme: 'Our addition, in some ways contrasting with, in other ways analogous to, the original block, is inevitably awkward perhaps, and shows a not too obvious respect for the past. In Italian piazzas similar juxtapositions developed over time in the dense architectural complexes that we admire so much; those complexes make up in guts for what they lose in composition. But our impulse to juxtapose the new with the old in this way came primarily not from an aesthetic preference, but from particular determinants of the site and program. The only site for the new wing was a narrow sloping strip of land between the Museum and the adjacent Hall Auditorium; there was no room for extension on the north side or in the back.'

Allen Memorial Art Museum
west elevation with addition
and renovation by Venturi and Rauch
1974
Contact print on positive film
with pantone
15 × 51½ in (38.1 × 130.8 cm)
Allen Memorial Art Museum
Oberlin College

The *Giant Three-Way Plug, Scale A, 1/3*,
in front of the addition by Venturi and
Rauch to Cass Gilbert's Allen Memorial
Art Museum in Oberlin, after reinstallation
of the *Plug* in the Fall of 1976.

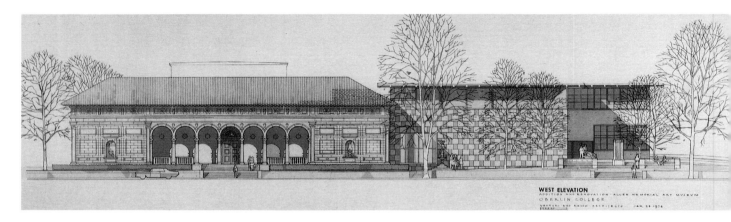

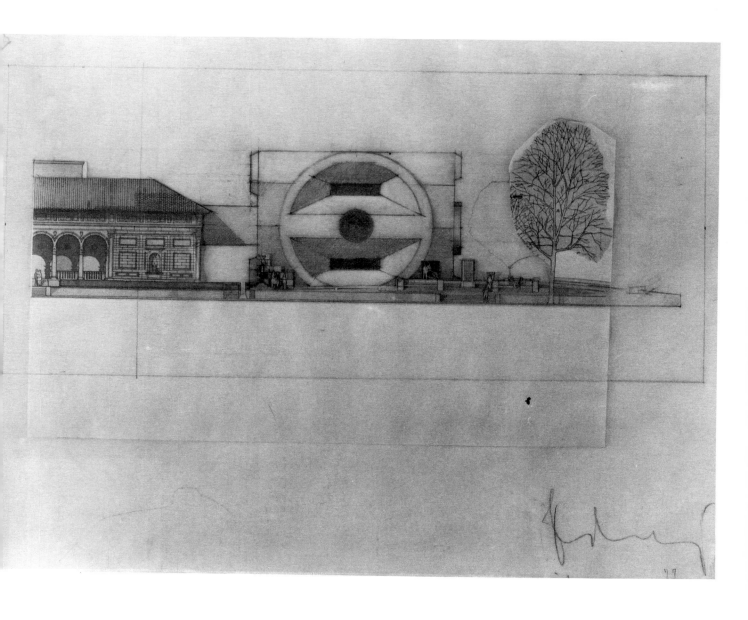

Notebook Page: Design for a Mathematics
Building at Yale University
New Haven, October 1969
Pencil, clipping
11 × 8½ in (28 × 21.6 cm)

Another kind of three-way plug, in a
brutalist modern style.
References are made to other buildings
in the New Haven area.

10/69

for yale.

– Knights of Col.
  tower
– building by long
      what:
    alcoa?

122

The development of a plug into a building is a logical step within Oldenburg's work. As early as 1967 English and Swedish extension plugs were expanded into functional buildings: the English one became a crematorium and the Swedish one, because of its vaulted cross construction, a chapel.
'A plug is so architectural to begin with, following it to the conclusion of a building is easy. A functional part in a plug becomes a functional part in a building (the outlets become windows, the prongs stairwells, etc.). An object and a building in the modern style change places easily.'

It certainly seems that way in the Plug-buildings or an *Alternative proposal for an addition to the Allen Memorial Art Museum, Oberlin, Ohio*. The idea of a substitution of plug for building occurred to Oldenburg in October 1976, when he re-sited the *Giant 3-Way Plug* near the addition to the Allen Art Museum by Venturi and Rauch.

In the etching the sculpture of the *Giant 3-Way Plug* has replaced the addition, becoming a colossal plug or an architectural structure, while the Venturi and Rauch wing is reduced to the scale of a sculpture, becoming a rather unidentifiable box-like shape. The juxtaposition of the Allen Art Museum in a Renaissance style and the Plug-buildings in the form of a banal, contemporary object seems, according to Venturi's theory, to enhance each of them through contrast. A similar opposition was applied by Oldenburg within the design of the Plug-buildings themselves; a balance is achieved between universal, geometric shapes and the stereotypical organization of these elements which makes them recognizable as a plug. The design of the Plug-buildings matches and contrasts with the Allen Art Museum just as the sculpture of the *Giant 3-Way Plug* does. Although Oldenburg was not bound to a building programme, the possibility of adding Plug-buildings in any direction linked by their prong 'corridors' was a practical solution for expansion of the Museum.

Despite the enormous shift in scale from real to colossal, one's recognition of a plug could give the building a look of intimate familiarity. On the other hand, the proposal could be an ungraspable and surprising curiosity, reminiscent of the description in Jonathan Swift's *Voyage to Lilliput* of two diminutive people finding the pocket-pistol of the man-mountain Gulliver:
'In the large pocket of the right side of his middle cover ... we saw a hollow pillar of iron about the length of a man, fastened to a strong piece of timber, larger than the pillar; and upon one side of the pillar were huge pieces of iron sticking out, cut into strange figures, which we know not what to make of.'

For the time being, the alternative proposal will remain in the realm of unfeasible projects. Faced with Oldenburg's vision one has to identify oneself with Gulliver, looking down at a Lilliputian world and seeing Plug-buildings rendered in a scale close to that of an actual plug.

Published in *Claes Oldenburg: Large-Scale Projects, 1977–1980, A Chronicle by Coosje van Bruggen & Claes Oldenburg*, New York, 1980, pp. 38–43.
1. Ellen Johnson, 'Oldenburg's Giant 3-Way Plug', *Allen Memorial Art Museum Bulletin*, XXVIII, 1970–71, p. 226.
2. *Allen Memorial Art Museum Bulletin*, XXXIV, no. 2, 1976–77, pp. 90–91.

Proposed Chapel in the Form
of a Swedish Extension Plug
1967
Crayon and watercolour on paper
22 × 30 in (55.9 × 76.2 cm)
Collection Krannert Art Museum
University of Illinois, Champaign

*Building in the Form of an English
Extension Plug*
1967
Pencil on paper
22 × 30 in (55.9 × 76.2 cm)
Collection James Fleck
Willowdale, Ontario

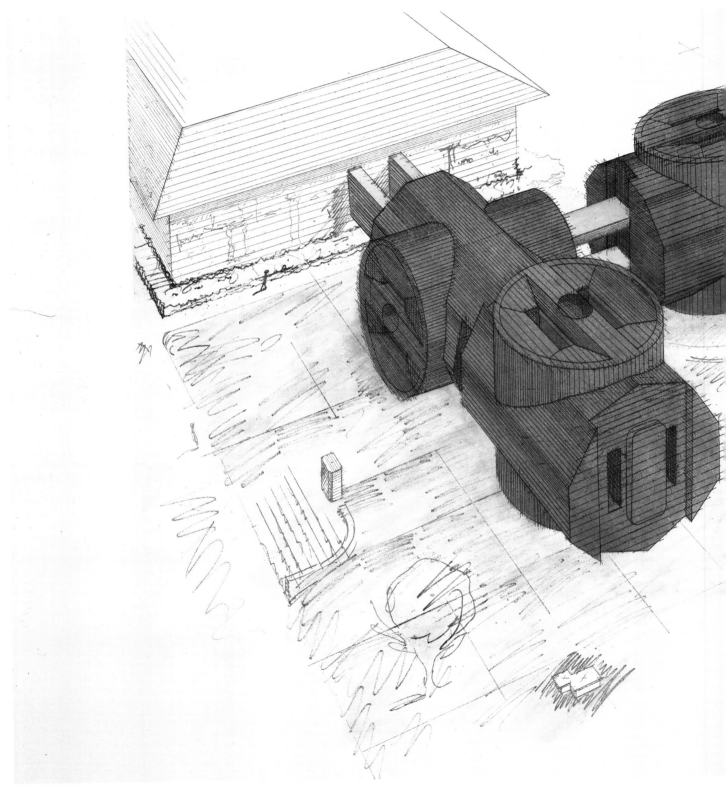

An Alternate Proposal for an Addition to the Allen Memorial Art Museum
1979
Hard and soft-ground etching
with aquatint
33⅞ × 36⁹⁄₁₆ in (86 × 93 cm)
Printed at Aeropress, New York
by Pat Branstead, Gretchen Gelb
and Sally Sturman
Published by Multiples, Inc, New York

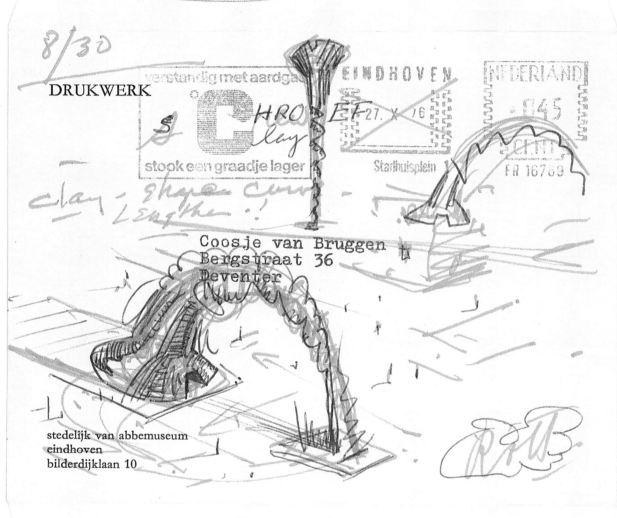

Tive ad. Hannover.

8/30

DRUKWERK

Coosje van Bruggen
Bergstraat 36
Deventer

stedelijk van abbemuseum
eindhoven
bilderdijklaan 10

EINDHOVEN

NEDERLAND
.045
FR 16789

Screwarch

Facing page:
*Notebook Page: Sketch of Screwarch
for the Churchillplein, Rotterdam*
August 1976
Felt pen, ball-point pen on envelope
Envelope 9¾ × 6 in (24.8 × 15.2 cm)
from sheet 11 × 8½ in (28 × 21.6 cm)

In the Wake of the Screwarch

Claes Oldenburg

The screw is among the super-ordinary, ubiquitous objects of this world, like the butt, the match, and the nail. It began in Los Angeles and is a sort of insignia of the kinetic object period. Its first step into another scale than itself was its identification with the palm trees of Los Angeles. The screw developed in two directions: as pure shape and as shape in combination with function. As shape, the screw entered the range of forms which include the tornado (a soft screw in itself), the *Tongue Cloud*, the ice cream cone and the cocktail, though from the beginning there were two types of heads on the screw, flat and rounded, the latter more appropriate to its identification with a palm. It mutated into balloons and buildings, all rendered in drawings and prints, with the exception of the *Soft Screw*, 1969. As a functioning object the screw has one possibility only: a simple, rotating rising and falling motion which relates it to the *Lipstick* or *Drill Bit*. There is a special category of softness in the case of the screw which consists in casting the hard form in soft material, different from the usual procedure of rebuilding a piece in cloth or vinyl. This produces a hard and soft combination which in the screw is best expressed when it takes the form of an arc tending towards an arch, a supremely unfunctional contradiction of the object's original purpose. If this version of a screw has to function at all it has to try to become a bridge.

Study for a Soft Screw
1969
Painted canvas, wire on a wooden base
$10^{5}/_{8} \times 7 \times 3^{1}/_{2}$ in ($27 \times 18 \times 9$ cm)

Notebook Page: Soft Screw in Waterfall
and Screw/Tornado/Searchlights
Los Angeles, 1968
Ball point pen, watercolour
Two sheets 6⅞ × 4¾ in (16.2 × 12.1 cm)
2¾ × 5 in (12.7 × 7 cm)
on sheet 11 × 8½ in (28 × 21.6 cm)

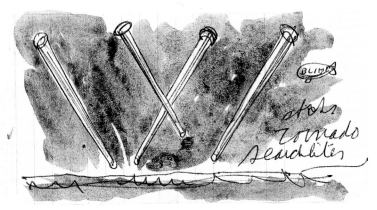

Rising and Falling Screw
1969
Cardboard and wood, painted
with spray enamel: pencil
$11 \times 28 \times 10^{7}/_{16}$ in
($28 \times 71 \times 26.5$ cm)

First try at the subject, in schematic form,
showing the adaptability of cardboard to
imagery. As in the case of the *Three-Way
Plug*, one knows what is concealed. This
proposal was suggested for a site somewhere
in Los Angeles, where the screw would
signify the time of day: down at midnight, up
at noon, when the screw would rival the palm
trees all around.

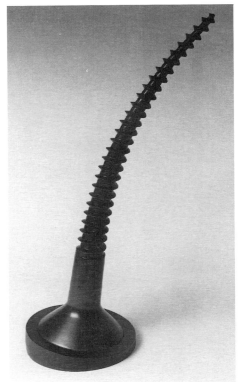

Mechanical model of *Rising and Falling Screw*
1969
Plastic and aluminum
Maximum height 98½ in (2.5 m)
Screw 47¼ in (120 cm)
Collection Gemini G.E.L.
Los Angeles

Gemini G.E.L. had a prototype built based on my drawing of an ideal screw, which rose and fell within an aluminium cage, releasing red oil in the highest position.
The full-scale version, to stand near their office, was never built. Instead the prototype was translated into soft plastic and, later, into the curved bronze castings of the *Screwarch Bridge Model.*

Bridge over the Rhine at Düsseldorf
in the Shape of a Colossal Saw
1971
Pencil, crayon on paper
11 × 14½ in (27.8 × 37 cm)

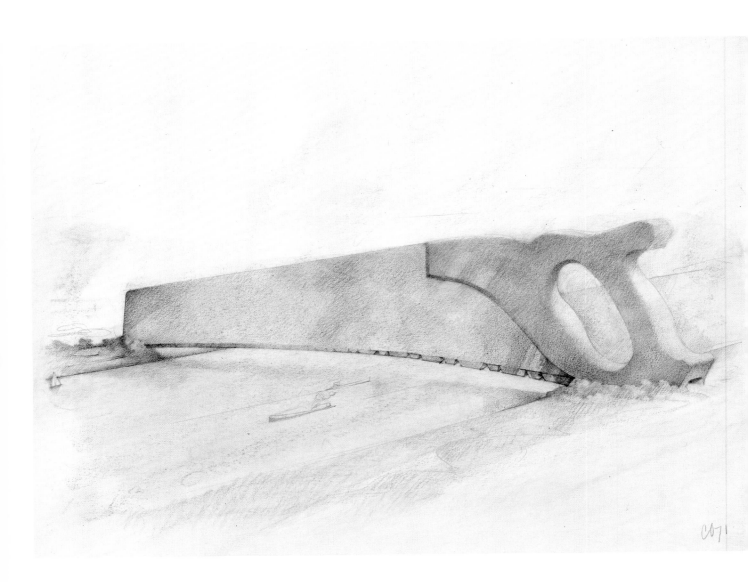

Cemetery in the Shape of a Colossal Screw: Skyscraper for São Paolo, Brazil
1971
Pencil and crayon on paper
14½ × 11 in (37 × 27.8 cm)

I read in the paper that there was such a shortage of cemetery space in São Paolo, Brazil, that high-rise structures were being planned to accommodate the overpopulation of the dead. These vertical cemeteries in the form of a screw would be scattered around the city, in different stages of descent. When filled, the round head of the screw would project above the ground as a marker or monumental structure.

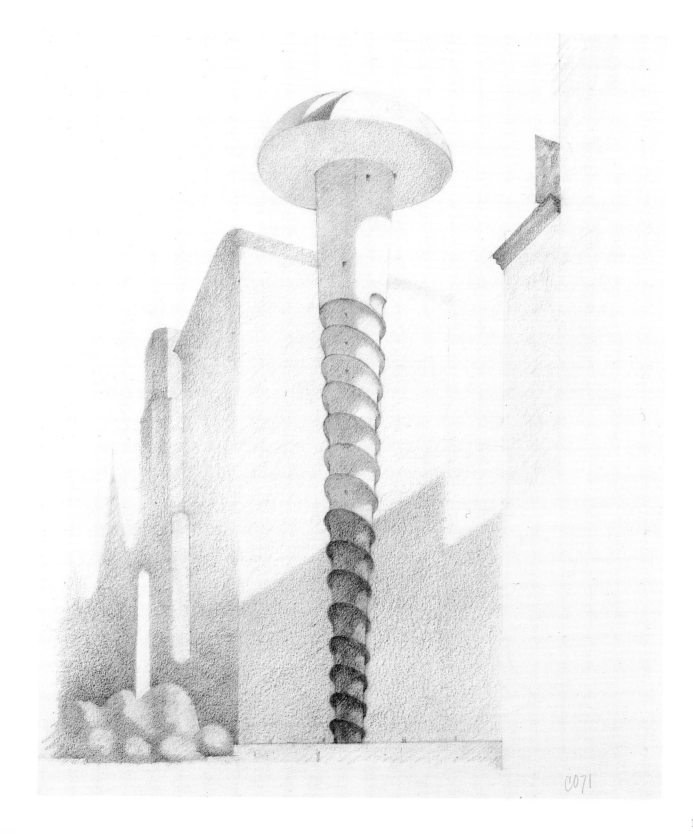

135

*Notebook Page: Bridge for Duisburg,
Derived from an Inverted Elephant Head*
June 1975
Pencil, ball-point pen
Sheet 2¾ × 5 in (7 × 12.6 cm) detail
from sheet 11 × 8½ in (28 × 21.6 cm)

The drawing was occasioned by word of a commission for a new bridge over the Rhine at Duisburg. The form of the bridge, an antecedent of the *Screwarch Bridge*, is an extension into three dimensions of the combined profiles of an elephant's head and a plume of smoke.

The tusks turn into smokestacks, the most prominent landmarks of the city. 'Brücke' of course is a loaded term in German art history. I refer to Barry Flanagan because the form of the bridge reminded me of some carpet-roll or sausage-like pieces of his I had seen.

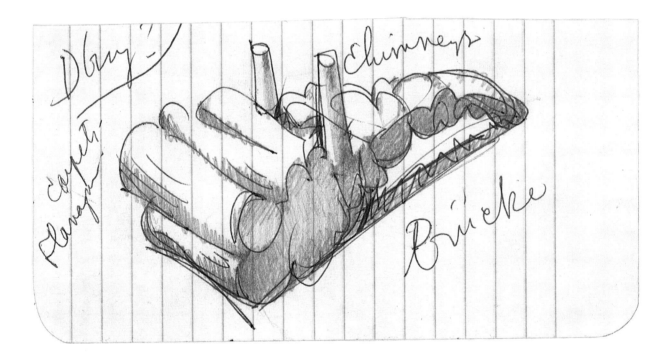

Soft Screw as Balloon, Ascending, A.C.II
1976
Lithograph
67½ × 45 in (171.5 × 114.3 cm)
Published by Gemini G.E.L., Los Angeles
Edition of 35

Arched Soft Screw as Building, A.C.II
1976
Lithograph
67½ × 45 in (171.5 × 114.3)
Published by Gemini G.E.L., Los Angeles
Edition of 35

*Notebook Page: Study for a Model
of the Screwarch Bridge*
July 1979
Crayon, pencil, watercolour
Sheet 5⅛ × 8½ in (13 × 21.5 cm)
from sheet 11 × 8½ in (28 × 21.6 cm)

The question was whether the *Screwarch Bridge* was to be an office building as well, like the *Saw Bridge* over the Rhine, in which case window recesses would have to be made in the mould. The proposal of the *Screwarch* for a site in Cleveland in 1976 was turned down out of fear of the inevitable exploitation by the press of the term 'screw.' In Holland the name was no obstacle. Besides, the *Screwarch*, which looked arbitrary in Times Square and was merely formal in Cleveland (it was succeeded by a Tony Smith), had an appropriate, indigenous look in Holland, first because the arch defines a horizontal plane and second because you can't go very far in Holland before you need a bridge. Knowing my fascination with bridges, Coosje gave me a book on Amsterdam's bridges when I arrived in Holland in 1976.

crewarch Model, A.P. 1/1
977–78
ronze
7¾ × 31 × 11 in
5 × 78.7 × 28 cm)
dition of 4

Screw shaped pumps are used to raise water from one level to another throughout The Netherlands. This example was photographed at Kinderdijk, near Rotterdam, 3 December 1977. The chance discovery of these devices was one of those coincidences which seem to assure the rightness of a subject for its site. A relation to the 'screws' of the shipping in the harbour had already been established but this clinched it. These particular pumps also suggested a scale and a means of fabrication.

Screwarch Bridge Model
1980–81
Bronze, aluminium and plastic; painted
19¹³⁄₁₆ × 99⁹⁄₁₆ × 44¹³⁄₁₆ in
(50.5 × 253 × 114 cm) on steel table
33 × 85¹³⁄₁₆ × 31¹⁄₁₆ in
(84 × 218 × 79 cm)
Museum Boymans-van Beuningen
Rotterdam

In 1978, the Director of the Boymans-van
Beuningen Museum, Wim Beeren, wished to
commission an in-depth group of works from
selected contemporary artists. For my
contribution, Coosje suggested several works
in different scales and techniques on the
theme of the Screwarch, including
documentation on the bridge proposal for
Rotterdam.

Larger proposals are of two sorts, unfeasible or feasible. But in the case of the *Screwarch Bridge*, the distinction is deliberately blurred; every effort was made to support the feasibility of the impossible. The proposal was identified with an actual project in process and Coosje and I proceeded as if our version was the one to be realized. In fact, it took longer to complete the etching of our proposal than it took the City of Rotterdam to construct a bridge, which I heard they bought ready-made from Germany. At the same time, the subject was pursued in a more feasible way, culminating in the 12½ foot high *Screwarch* which became part of the commission by the Boymans-van Beuningen Museum.

Double Screwarch Bridge
1981
State II: etching with aquatint
State III: etching with aquatint
and monotype
31½ × 58 in (80 × 147.3 cm)
Printed at Aeropress, New York
by Pat Branstead and Young Soon Min
Published by Multiples, Inc, New York

The drawing which culminated in the
Screwarch Bridge etching was begun in 1978,
along the lines of the colossal monument
proposals, using an epic scale not literally
descriptive of the Rotterdam site. The etching
aimed at an identification with the visionary
technique of the seventeenth century Dutch
artist and printmaker Hercules Seghers.

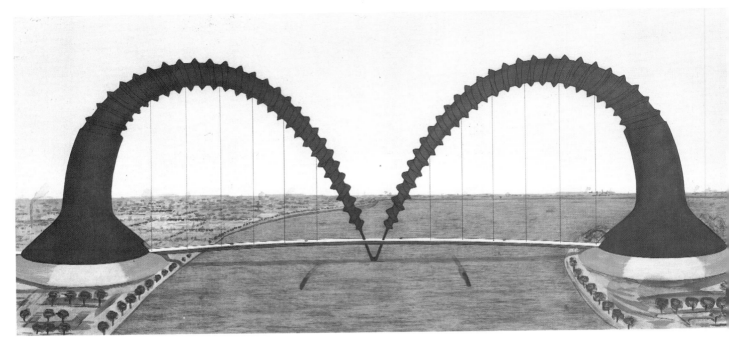

Warmup Landscapes
1981
Colour monoprints
Four, each 10⅝ × 14½ in (27 × 37 cm)
Küpferstichkabinett, Oeffentliche
Kunstsammlung, Basel

The landscape surrounding the *Screwarch Bridge* (State III) and the texture of its bases was done as a monoprint, by applying ink directly to the plate and differently for each print in the edition. Since correction of the large plates would be laborious, the printer, Pat Branstead, decided to provide me with smaller plates for testing the brushes and the consistency of pigmentation of the inks, as well as the quality of the attack.

The only consistency in these preparatory or 'warmup' plates was the viewpoint, from a plane presumably, approaching the landscape at the same altitude as in the print. To make the warmup process more interesting I imagined that the plane was flying over landscapes in different parts of the world.

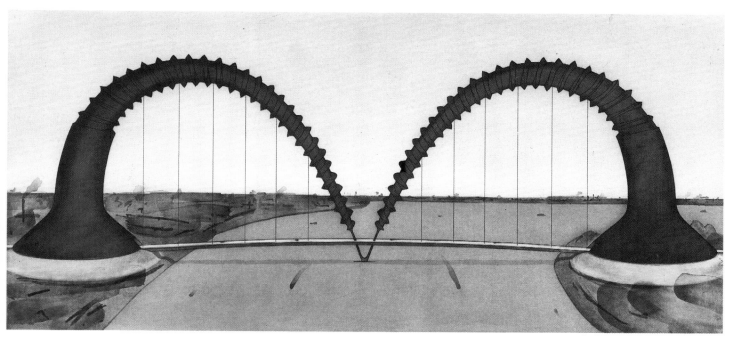

Screwarch
1983
Aluminium, painted
152 × 257⅞ in (386 × 655 cm)
Boymans-van Beuningen
Rotterdam, The Netherlands

Five years later, the Museum presented the results of the commission: the two prints, the model and its plans, and the 12½ foot high *Screwarch*, with related studies. In 1986, the large *Screwarch* was shifted to a site outdoors which Coosje and I selected to maintain the relationship to water and suggest the function of a bridge.

Berlin

USA

" The cream style "

Cross-Section
of a Toothbrush

Facing page:
Notebook Page: Toothbrush with Paste
March 1969
Pencil, coloured pencil, clipping
Clipping 7⅜ × 5¼ in (18.7 × 13.3 cm)
on sheet 11 × 8½ in (28 × 21.6 cm)
Proposal for a sculpture in plastic about 12
feet high, to be sited on a slope. The handle
would be eliminated. The paste form would
apotheosize the passionate representations
of cream of all kinds in American ads (Claes
Oldenburg, *Notes in Hand*, 1971, no. 41).

Cross-section

Claes Oldenburg

The toothbrush had been a prominent object in art of the 1960s, appearing for example in works by Jasper Johns and Jim Dine. George Brecht once presented me with an oversize toothbrush from a 'Dr. West' display (now in the Mouse Museum), but I never tried the subject. Instead, I was attracted by the paste and tube part of the complex. For example, in the notebook page published in *Notes in Hand*, the focus is on the paste, as a symbol of *The U.S.A. Cream Style*. I saw the tube as my double in object form, as in the series of drawings begun in 1969 titled *Tube Supported by its Contents*, and the sculptural version of the theme constructed in Düsseldorf in 1985.

The choice of the toothbrush as a subject was undoubtedly stimulated by my wife and partner, Coosje van Bruggen's interest in conceptual and minimal form. I remember us both admiring a work by the Californian sculptor John McCracken in the Kröller-Müller collection: a blue bar of perfectly smooth surface which formed a diagonal against the wall of the museum and, in retrospect, could serve as an equivalent for the toothbrush handle in its rest position on our bathroom sink. Thus from the start the subject was associated with Coosje's viewpoint; I eventually came to identify the toothbrush as much with her as I identified the tube with myself.

The development of the toothbrush, in its cup, into a sculpture began in September 1980. At the time I was using a particular toothbrush and cup. The handle was blue with curved contours; a tip of natural rubber for massaging the gums was attached to the end. The cup was of red plastic with soft edges and the toothbrush was usually stored in it, brush downward.

In the first attempt at a sculpture, this familiar part of the domestic landscape was combined with a clipping from an advertisement which showed a toothbrush with the brush part up standing in a glass so clear that only the bottom and the rim were visible. This led to the concept of an invisible glass, suggested by a ring above, attached to the diagonal handle of the toothbrush which was in turn attached to another ring at the bottom, the three elements forming a version of the percent sign.

Soon however the sculpture acquired a more specific character as it merged with our thinking in relation to a particular site on the campus of the University of Hartford in Connecticut. Hartford made us think of the poet Wallace Stevens who had lived and worked in the city; a dormitory on the campus had been named for him. Stevens and William Carlos Williams were the modern American poets that Coosje liked best. Besides their poetry, we were interested by the fact that both had led double lives, Williams as a physician, Stevens as an insurance salesman, which had made them question the relation of art to life, imagination to reality, one of the central concerns of our approach.

We associated three particular poems by Stevens with the toothbrush in a cup: *Anecdote of the Jar*, which evokes the image of a large-scale container, like a cup, set in a landscape; *Of Hartford in a Purple Light*, which concerns the passage of the sun and the effects of light on the landscape; and *So-And-So Reclining on Her Couch*, which interweaves the human body with geometry, particularly the triangle. The last-named poem also contains the term 'Gothic prong' which we equated with the onion-shaped blue dome of the Colt gun factory, a prominent landmark in Hartford, and with the Victorian Gothic architecture for which the city is known, as well as the rubber tip of the toothbrush.

Notebook Page: Toothbrush
in Glass = percent sign
September 1980
Pencil, ball-point pen
Two sheets, 4 × 2¾ in (10.2 × 7 cm)
and 5 × 2¾ in (12.8 × 7 cm), detail from
sheet 11 × 8½ in (28 × 21.6 cm)

Two circles with a connecting diagonal also
form the structure of the bow tie and the
Tilting Neon Cocktail.

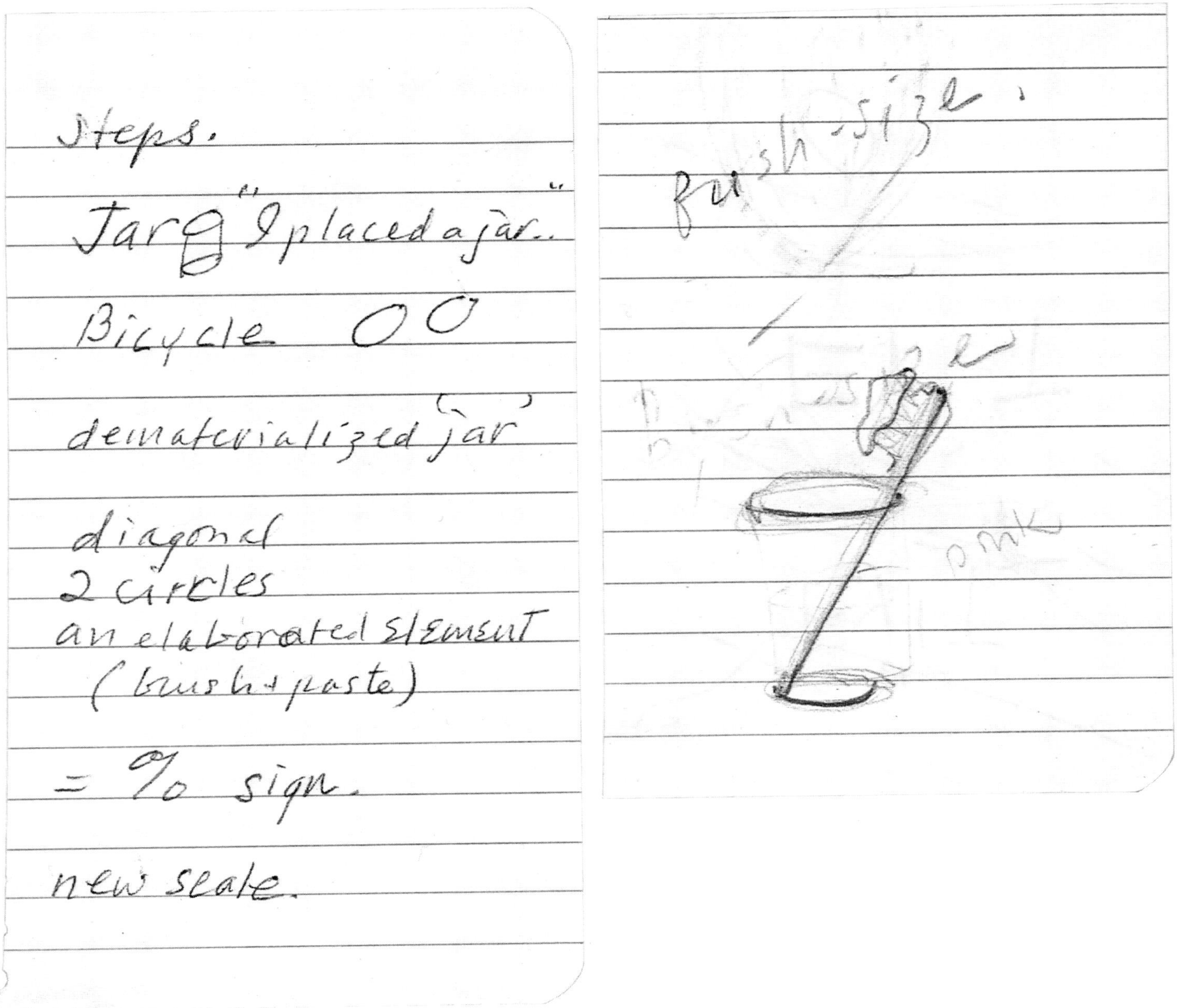

steps.

Jar "I placed a jar.

Bicycle   O O

dematerialized jar

diagonal
2 circles
an elaborated element
(brush + paste)

= % sign.

new scale.

brush-size.

pink

Notebook Page: Cross-section of
Toothbrush in Glass, 'sun dial'
October–November 1980
Ball-point pen, felt pen
11 × 8½ in (28 × 21.6 cm)

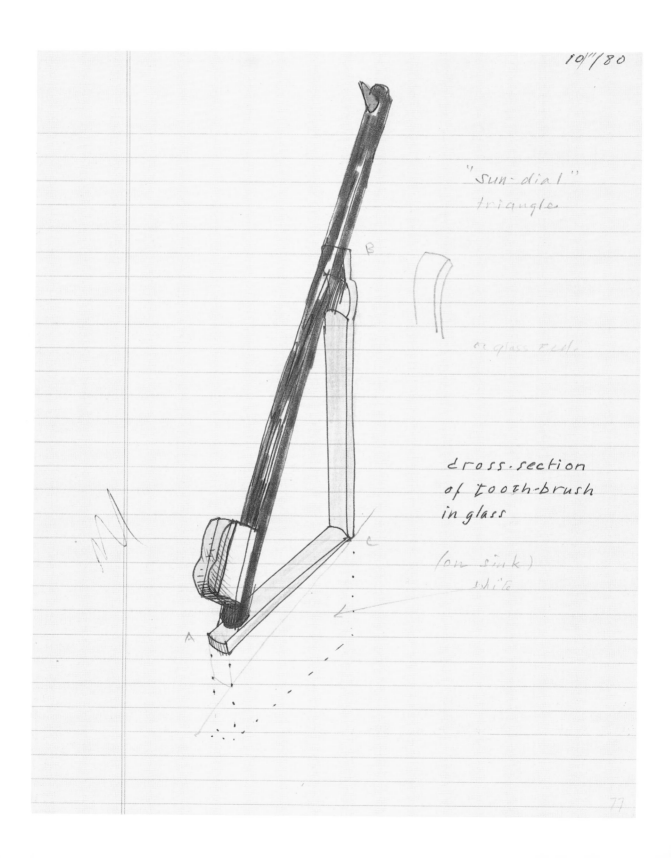

"sun-dial"
triangle

cross-section
of tooth-brush
in glass

(on sink)

Notebook Page: Sign on a Street in Hartford Connecticut, October 1980
Snapshot 3½ × 5 (9 × 12.5 cm) detail from sheet 11 × 8½ in (28 × 21.6 cm)

These associations produced another formulation of the sculpture, made by nailing and gluing together fragments of wood and paper found in the studio. The rim of the cup disappeared; besides the bottom, all that remained was a segment of the side of the cup as wide as the handle of the toothbrush. The segment was set at a 90 degree angle to the bottom; with the handle it formed a triangle that suggested a sun-dial.

In discussing this model, Coosje was less interested in the sun-dial effect than in what she perceived as a slice through the handle and the cup. It would be two parallel slices in fact; one could imagine that they had trimmed the curves from the handle and left just the segment of the cup. In this model the slices stopped short of the bottom of the cup. In response to Coosje's perception I made a drawing which emphasized the sliced effect more by continuing it through the bottom and into a base identifiable as a section of a sink.

The drawing of this stage shows the sculpture as both a sun-dial and a cross-section. A, B, C identifies the points of the triangle from the Stevens poem *So-And-So Reclining . . .* Whatever lies outside the cut is discarded.

The toothbrush group is what Coosje and I call a cluster, the presentation of several objects together. Previous clusters have included deliberate groupings of objects such as servings of food on a plate and accidental juxtapositions such as the fragments of window displays and advertisements shown in *The Store.* The reduction of several contiguous objects to a single form by cutting through them was a new approach to presenting such a cluster. Following a notepage drawing which defined the scale, I built another model, in cardboard. The slice of sink, higher and now hollow (as a real sink would be) was equated with the angular shape of a roadside sign I had seen in Hartford.

The uniqueness of the piece seemed to lie not so much in the use of certain objects as in what was done to them, and so the subject, stated in the title, became: a cross-section. In engineering terminology, a cross-section is usually a horizontal cut rather than a vertical one. However the word was chosen more for its general connotation and for its sound in relation to the rest of the title: *Cross-section of a Toothbrush with Paste, in a Cup, on a Sink.* A cadence suggestive of one of Lawrence Weiner's conceptual pieces was evoked deliberately.

In its allusions to other art, the sculpture reflected Coosje's profession of art historian. These allusions were primarily to cubism and constructivism, two of her favorite areas of study. The colour scheme was reminiscent of the Dutch flag (she was born in Groningen), and also reminded me of the red sweater and blue jeans I had often seen her wear when we lived in Deventer in an earlier period. Moreover the sculpture seemed to suggest Coosje's physique, an association she confirmed, commenting that like her body the sculpture was 'bony, with little soft parts'. One evening, struck with how much of Coosje was contained in the sculpture I offered to 'dedicate' the work to her. Coosje replied that she did not believe in dedications and besides that her contribution to the work transcended the role of a muse: she was responsible for the idea of the cross-section which gave the work its special identity. In fact she had applied to the sculpture her approach to any subject as reflected in her writing style: an analytical approach cutting through a context to reveal the relation of its parts. Also she spoke appreciatively of the

Notebook Page: Desk Pen and Cookie Cutter Rabbit
September 1980
Pencil, ball-point pen
Two sheets 5 × 2¾ in
(12.8 × 7 cm)
on sheet 11 × 8½ in
(28 × 21.6 cm)

The desk pen is a ready-made monument of the eternal flame variety, usually equipped with an ostentatious marble base. It seemed too cruel a comparison to make: the poet and insurance underwriter, but the strong diagonal stayed in the later concept of the *Cross-section of a Toothbrush*.

The search for a representation of a rabbit suitable for development into a sculpture led to a cookie cutter contour, freely re-drawn, with exaggerated ears, which was later realized in the *Calico Bunny*.

'radical, decisive, surgical' character of the slice and compared the pink paste and brown tip to the 'little exotic details' which she liked to include in her writing. In view of the importance of her participation and its autographic character, I suggested amplifying the title by adding: *Portrait of Coosje's Thinking*. She was reminded of *Le Penseur* by Rodin (there is no Penseuse) and commented that this sculpture would certainly be the first which commemorated a woman's thinking.

The sculpture has been called an untypical Oldenburg work. This is not accurate if one places the *Toothbrush* in the line of works beginning in 1963 whose choice of subject, from a home environment, and treatment were influenced by the requirements of fabrication, first in wood (for example, the *Ping Pong Table* or *Light Switches*) and later in metal (such as the *Clothespin*). But it is true in that the *Toothbrush* is the first large-scale polychromed outdoor work and, most importantly, in that it is a deliberately collaborative work in which the terms of collaboration are strikingly evident. The title might have been: *Self-portrait of Coosje's Thinking*. To me this only adds to the complexity and interest of the work.

To identify the sculpture with thinking was not inconsistent with the Stevens subject. Human thinking itself often seems the subject of his poems, more than the many sensuous objects and impressions that become its agents and devices. But not very much about the appearance of the sculpture at this stage evoked Stevens. In a more Stevens-like direction, we had considered the following subjects: a bow-tie bridge, a desk-set with a diagonal pen, an over-size cookie-cutter in the shape of a bunny (a response to the poem *A Rabbit as King of the Ghosts*) and especially a pair of tied sneaker-laces, rising like a palm tree which Coosje found more appropriate to Stevens' convoluted sensibility than the Rietveld-like rigour of the *Toothbrush in a Cup*. However none of these directions had been developed into practical sculptural terms, and now the Hartford deadline was upon us.

The *Toothbrush* was ready to be realized as a large-scale sculpture and though it had taken off in its own direction we felt that enough associations with the Hartford situation remained to justify proposing it for the University of Hartford campus. We visited the campus and selected a site on the bank of the Park river, along a road that led from the dormitories to the classrooms. The students would encounter the *Toothbrush* from one side in the morning and from the other in the evening. In the landscape as in the home it stood not far from water. I built another cardboard version of the sculpture slightly larger than the first in which the paste was placed diagonally across the brush and trimmed to conform to the slices of the rest. The parallel slices created a clearly marked zone so that, seen from the front and the back, the sculpture appeared to be a single line of varying colour areas. Dimensions were made specific for the translation into metal fabrication; the corrugated cardboard used to signify the brush would be imitated in aluminium in the larger version. On November 6, I returned to present this model to the President of the University and gathered officials. Coosje had pointed out that the toothbrush is one of the most intimate and evocative of the common objects in the home, one which figures especially in the relationship between men and women. The discussion which followed my presentation bore this out as I found it difficult to focus the attention of the committee on the sculpture itself: each member had a toothbrush story to get off their chest.

153

Notebook Page: Studies for a Sculpture
in the Form of a Sneaker
October 1980
Pencil
Two sheets 5 × 2¾ in (12.8 × 7 cm) detail
from sheet 11 × 8½ in (28 × 21.6 cm)

The subject goes back to a proposal for merging sneakers and palm trees in the edition of *Notes* published by Gemini G.E.L. in 1968 (no. IX). The title of Stevens' collection *The Palm at the End of the Mind*, may have aroused the connection with sneakers initially.

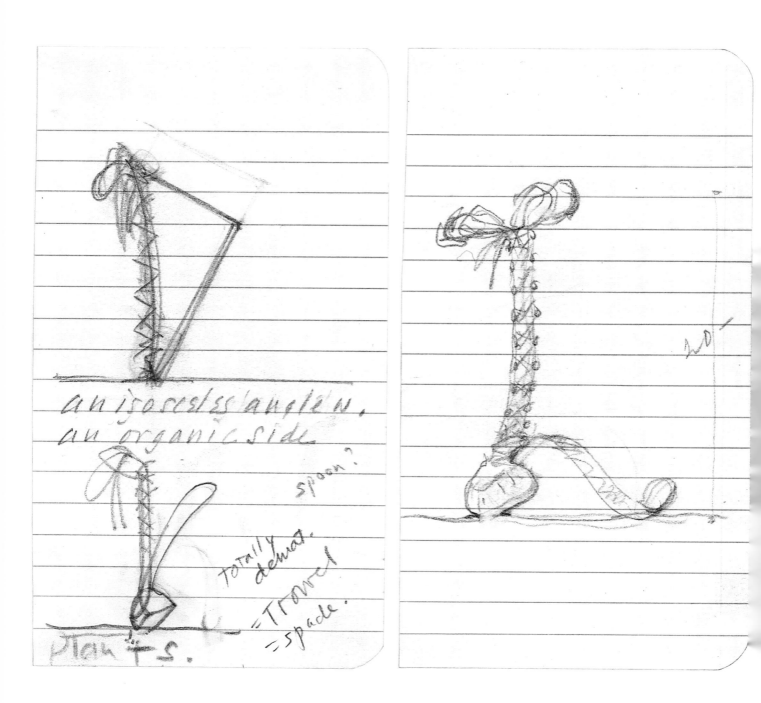

Elevations of *Cross-section of a*
Toothbrush with Paste, in a Cup,
on a Sink: Portrait of Coosje's Thinking
1983
Pencil
Drawn by J. Robert Jennings

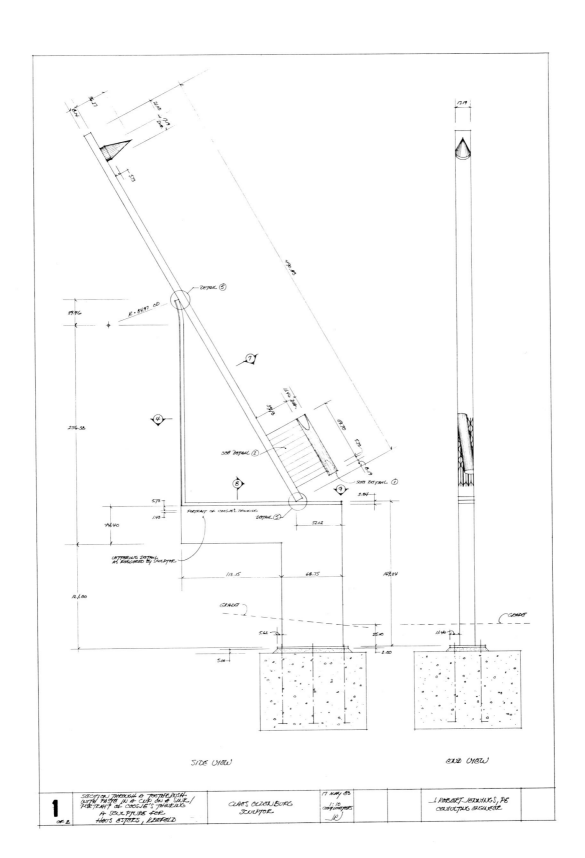

Cross-section of a Toothbrush
with Paste, in a Cup, on a Sink:
Portrait of Coosje's Thinking
1983
Steel, painted
6 m high
Haus Esters, Krefeld, West Germany

On March 21, 1981, the sculpture was rejected by the Board of Regents of the University 3 to 2, despite the recommendations of the University President, the Dean of the Art School, Brooks Atkinson, Director of the Wadsworth Athenaeum in the city and Alan Shestak, head of the Yale University Art Gallery. Half of the cost of the sculpture would have been paid by the United States government's National Endowment programme (NEA). Coming soon after the start of the Reagan administration, the rejection was viewed by the *New York Times* in a front page story as an indication of a negative attitude toward state sponsored public art.

Undiscouraged, and hoping to find another site for the sculpture, we met with our engineer J. Robert Jennings of North Madison, Connecticut, with whom we prepared plans based on the presentation model for a fabrication model nine feet high (2.74 m), made of aluminium. The model was built by Robert Giza at Malleable Metals in Bethany, Connecticut. I determined the exact colours at the Broome Street studio in New York in June 1982 and applied them in July at the San Francisco Museum of Modern Art, prior to the installation of the model in the exhibition Sculpture 1982.

In the beginning of June, on our way back from Documenta 7, Coosje and I stopped off in Krefeld to discuss with Gerhard Storck the possibility of a commission for the grounds of the Haus Esters to mark the 100th anniversary of the Krefelder Kunstverein. It was not until later in the year, when the model returned from the summer exhibition in San Francisco, that it occurred to us that the *Cross-section* might work in the Haus Esters site.

The sculpture was to have stood 23 feet (about 7 m) in the Hartford site, which was a scale roughly suitable to the Haus Esters and its surroundings; like Hartford, the Haus Esters site was a mixture of bricks and foliage.

Because the Haus Esters had originally been a home and still retained a residential character, the toothbrush seemed an appropriate emblem, the more so since artists-in-residence and a caretaker's family actually lived above the exhibition spaces. Stylistically, its constructivist character made it harmonious with the architecture, while clashing enough so as to maintain its individuality. The *Toothbrush* served as a foil to the building through its strong diagonal, its colours, its bizarre details, its changeability dependent on one's viewpoint and above all its pop conception, which might offend the neighbours on the conservative, steel-shuttered Wilhelmshofallee.

Gerhard Storck visited the Broome Street studio in November 1982 and on the basis of the nine foot model chose the *Cross-section* for the Haus Esters site. I could not suppress my feeling that after many diversions the sculpture had finally found its true destination, completely unforeseen at the beginning of the project.

Published in *Claes Oldenburg: Cross Section of a Toothbrush with Paste in a Cup on a Sink Portrait of Coosje's Thinking*, Krefelder Kunstmuseen, 1983, pp. 14–25.

Sculpture on the Borderline

Gerhard Storck

A sculpture, standing outdoors, is subject to its own laws. It must take everything which happens around it into account. Outdoors there is little to rely on. Every freedom including the escape from the artistic atmosphere of the museum has its price.

The first commandment as regards outdoor survival is resistance to the weather. Stone and metal, above all marble and bronze, have always been considered as the most useful materials, for the open air. In the past, terracotta was a cheap substitute, now polyester is being used. These products, however, lack true hardness. Although this is present in concrete, there is already quite enough of it about, in the opinion of perceptive contemporaries. Therefore few artists are tempted to create something outdoors with this amorphous material.

As far as the artist is concerned, the material is, of course, absolutely vital. How else could he express his ideas and experiences? The observer, however, is above all interested in the form and only peripherally in the material. The same is true of the artist but he approaches it from the opposite angle. After all it is he who has to force his way through to a decision which we perceive ready-made. All previous considerations and sketches, ideas and contradictions, details and corrections may amount to an interesting history, which in turn may help in explaining the vitality of a piece; the inner life of a sculpture, however, is not affected by such considerations. The pre-history of a sculpture may be thrilling, but what is decisive is what we finally see.

The sculptor, who would like to attract our attention amidst today's chaos, is doubly taxed. For despite all his love for the intangible, which is concealed in every work of art, he must never lose sight of the tangible. The interior sculptor may, like the painter, now and then come out with allusions. The sculptor, who sees the outside as his place of work, must always create clear facts, even if he has a multitude of meanings at heart. This means in effect that the sculptor has to set standards outside, which take care of the indefinite, but do not create the type of order which excludes all movement. And thus we have finally arrived at the theme: the sculptures of Claes Oldenburg in general and his *Cross-section of a Toothbrush* in particular.

There is a magic word which Claes Oldenburg always has ready when discussing his sculpture. The word is '*scale*'. The artist utters this word in such a way that all things externally come into motion. With the varying scales of their apparent forms they must then by necessity look around for a motive for their changed form of existence. The artist, however, helps them in their search for a new existence: because whoever says '*mutabor*' must take the consequences. Claes Oldenburg assists the transformed objects by searching and turning over pages in his thousand and one memories in order to find suitable connections. In this collection of most diverse impressions of reality, which are daily supplemented by new aspects, it is a question of an open plan of creation which at once takes human weakness into consideration. Thus we are at liberty to laugh. Above all, this all-embracing plan takes into account the revolt of the underprivileged objects of everyday life of a civilised continent, in which three forms of nature are in conflict and are striving towards equality. The first is all that could survive better without civilised humans. This one is still, possibly, the soul of America. Number two is the outcome of the interaction of all the methods and means created by humans. This could be described as the body of America. The third is the total

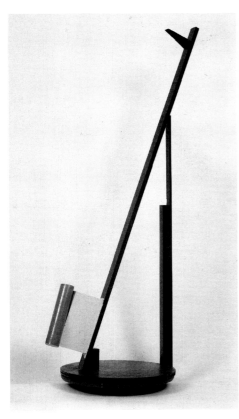

*Model of Cross-section of a Toothbrush
with Paste in a Cup*
1980
Wood, cardboard: enamel
59½ × 22½ × 18¼ in
(151.1 × 57.2 × 46.4 cm)

of pictures, substitutes and publicity campaigns. This third nature, is the mirror of America. And now this illusion would like to merge body and soul in one.

Here the artist makes his appearance. He knows by experience how to handle artificial things. Since he is aware of the fact that he cannot turn back the wheel of history only one way remains open; to express his sense of what is genuine in the middle of all this trivia. He must help to give stature and greatness to even the most obvious of everyday gadgets, which today appear as the most simple of natural objects and are therefore exploited by commerce as bearers of meaning. And he does this by implanting signs of the first and third nature, intrinsic value and symbolic value.

This may sound odd with regard to a sculpture like *Cross-section of a Toothbrush*. It may carry meaning besides being as self evident as a work of minimal or concept art. Above all, it is nothing complete. And where is the intrinsic value? Which ever way one looks at this work it is and remains a mixed creation. Neither a toothbrush nor an abstract construction, neither a purely plastic work nor a colourful drawing. And yet this sculpture asserts itself naturally outside. How come?

Well, she (sculpture is feminine!) exists by suggestion, by the openness of relations, by lacking unanimity in its external form. The unbreakable law of classical sculpture, which demands that a statue be able to roll down a hill and arrive at the bottom undamaged (a pointed nose could be at a disadvantage here), this law of a solid nucleus and external unanimity is literally turned upside down here. And yet, it is not a 'baroque' construction. Everything pointing to a hard interior is missing in this *Cross-section of a Toothbrush*. Even if looked at differently, there is little softness in this sculpture. Every detail points to geometry, is strictly linear. A linearity which not only appears colourful but which has also been developed around a toothbrush and which leaves no doubt that everything was defined precisely.

The sculpture stands like a perfect mannequin, like the picture or sketch of a clear yet not apprehended representation of an ideal. It does not demonstrate anything; it does not stimulatingly step past us. It stands silenly in front of us, making us believe it would constantly turn in front of our eyes. And yet it is we who circle around it incessantly, because we would like to know from which side we could best approach it. All the time one has the feeling that something is hidden. Looking straight from the side it is little more than an open triangle in slightly raised position. If one approaches directly from the front or rear it eludes our view, as if we could only see it through a small gap in a door. It keeps us at a distance; at the same time it is as transparent as an empty glass.

What is at once fascinating about this colourful sculpture which stands on the borderline of painting, drawing, construction and architecture, is its great self-sufficiency, which is based on nothing more than its open form. The construction does not appear unstable, despite its sensitive state of balance, which no one would dare touch. Remote from any form of external strength, leaning back, in a wait and see position, the sculpture puts all things around it in their proper place. Precisely fragile, colourful, spiced with a pinch of irony, it quietly creates the space of representation in order to reveal movement step by step. In '*us*', that is: we approach, stand, walk and wonder. It is indeed a matter of rubbing one's eyes. Can what we have before us really be true?

*Model of Cross-section of a Toothbrush
with Paste, in a Cup, on a Sink:
Portrait of Coosje's Thinking*
1981
Cardboard, wood, sand; painted
19 × 11¼ × 6⅝ in
(48.5 × 28.5 × 17 cm)

Obviously, this construction carries its whole sense in itself, and dares to be outdoors as a work of art. It stands so close to the road that it can hardly be ignored: it is indeed a sculpture in a public space.

Out here, on the periphery of the town and in the garden of a museum, this sculpture is only partially exposed to general taste. Yet it is nevertheless a touchstone for what is possible under special circumstances. Special circumstances in the case of art in a public space means private initiative; it follows therefore that the usual political committees have to some extent been relieved of their decision-making authority. For an evaluation of art out of doors no other guidelines can be used as standards than those indoors. In other words: without expert knowledge, one cannot manage outside either. However, in the case of an open air sculpture this is reduced, for reasons of acceptability, to a minimum. Because those responsible start with the assumption that a work of art in the street will only be 'accepted' by the citizens if it does not reveal itself as such and, above all, if it does not claim to influence ways of perception.

At least nine out of ten sculptures which are exhibited in public spaces have been ascertained by means of an act of balancing interests, whereby the main concern is to avoid 'excess'. But every important work of art is an 'excess', a clear step out of the familiar, a measure by which the familiar measure is transgressed. How else could works of art open our eyes to a way of looking at reality in which precisely what people would prefer to ignore begins to radiate a different light.

The problem in all art in public spaces lies in the false premise on which all the half-hearted measures are introduced. The starting point of a discussion is never if and how urban space can be made more evident through artistic means. From beginning to end, it is always a matter of how money donated from private means or via a law relating to a construction plan can be presented without disturbing the peace. In aesthetic circles, peace means normality: above all one wants to avoid disagreement about the meaning of something.

It is sad, but true: additional furnishing of our cities with 'pleasant art' makes them appear even more narrow than what is already provided by the usual embellishment. It is a false idea to start with the assumption that outside works of art have the function of filling empty spaces. On the contrary it is their function to make spaces comprehensible so that the inhabitants can take possession of them. They ought to take up so much space that the dainty rustic designs of the scattered 'extras' in the neighbourhood cease to exist. Art in public spaces: in the first instance this can only mean clearing out the cities, even if this goes against the grain of the experts in town planning, including the organised art establishment. Less outdoor art but in the right place and equipped with the right to open up channels to make the city transparent, that is the most important thing today.

The first task of a panel on Art in public space should therefore consist in preventing further refurbishment of streets and places with average art; the second task should be the working out of a plan of necessities and to provide breathing space; giving the re-gained space structure and effectively protecting it from interference of vested interests should be its third task. Only a convincing form can oppose constant fashion influences and create the sort of stability which we conceive as peaceful; the insignificant will subordinate

*Model of Cross-section of a Toothbrush
with Paste, in a Cup, on a Sink:
Portrait of Coosje's Thinking*
1981
Cardboard, wood, sand; painted
28 × 17¼ × 9¾ in
(71.1 × 43.8 × 24.8 cm)
Krefelder Kunstmuseen, Krefeld

itself easily to the main point. Such a conception of peace is the prerequisite for staying rather than escaping.

Let's stress it once more: in regaining urban space, the erection of a work of art is the last of necessary measures. A sculpture can only fulfil its purpose outside if the environment gives it stature. Its task is then to make use of its acquired importance. It must appear obvious why it is actually here, outside. But its function, from its special position, is to decisively further the human claim to a sensibly shaped environment. This means, however, that there is no general rule for what type of art should be given preference outside. The intended space can only give meaningful hints.

However, two things could be mentioned, if one wanted to formulate a hard and fast rule about what works of art in public spaces should generally fulfil in respect to form. First, they should be easily perceived and labelled even from a distance; secondly, they should not lose any attraction when seen close up (ie. when viewed consciously). This calculated mixture of formal generosity, which aids orientation, and pleasure in detail, which has an immediate beneficial effect on the senses, reads like a simple recipe. Yet for centuries this recipe has had a positive effect on open air sculpture, even if rather unconsciously, if by 'unconsciously' we understand 'naturally'. Opponents of 'classical' modern architecture may be amazed to learn that it was Walter Gropius who formulated this recipe early on for a renewal of architecture and town planning. Unfortunately one has scarcely followed this principle when re-building or 'renewing' our towns. Rather, it was thought sufficient on the one hand to have generous traffic-planning and brutally simple box-like architecture, and on the other hand a loving furnishing of the inhospitable spaces in between, in order to achieve a successful mix of opposing demands. But what was demanded by architects like Gropius, Mies van der Rohe or Le Corbusier, was a new architectonic structure, which unites those opposites.

But let's return to sculpture! *Cross-section of a Toothbrush* obviously fulfils the double demand, which was made above for an open air sculpture. In its basic form on the one hand it is easily graspable, on the other hand it lives close up through its details. Despite the long title, it suffices to speak of it as a 'Toothbrush' in order to understand it. It is precisely this modest actuality which joins the opposing aspects which become a matter of reflection in this open air sculpture.

Let's pretend that we cannot see independently, that we can only put art in its proper place with the aid of learned concepts of art history. At once there is an unsolvable problem. Because who could decide whether it is a work of so-called Pop Art or an expression of Minimal Art? If one also takes the title into consideration, the work comes close to Concept Art. From our own point of view, however, it is an unambiguous structure even if there is room for ambiguity. This sculpture is both simple and complex. It can be perceived directly, which is how it became popular so quickly, and one can discuss it in great detail, how it transgresses all forms of style operating between genres, how it establishes art historical relations (who, in view of the colour-construction is not automatically reminded of the Dutch 'Stijl' movement?) and even suggests everyday symbolism and biographic asides. But is this not all too much of a good thing for an open air sculpture? Is its energy not being dispersed by all these cross-references and is it no longer able to keep up with its main task, namely to dominate the space allotted to it outside? Yes and no.

First, no. What appears a cross-reference only marginally touches the external structure. It appears in the multi-coloured nature (which here belongs to detail), in the emphasis on a few individual forms, which can be explained 'naturally', or on geometry, which could be a matter of being conditioned by the material; and is present in the title, which need not necessarily be known in order to find the work pleasing. The decisive point is that the sculpture, viewed up close, offers enough circumstantial aspects in order to be enticing in the long term, and that it remains a simple geometrical structure: or just an over-sized toothbrush.

Now to the affirmative, the doubts whether this multi-dimensional 'picture' is not after all misplaced in the open. I'm not concerned about the observer who may be out of his depth. As pointed out already, the simple path is levelled for him; he can apprehend the subject as what it suddenly reveals itself to be. Yes, it is a toothbrush, not a flight of bronze ducks pretending to gather around a fountain, and admittedly this is supposed to be a matter of art rather than mere 'acceptance'. Nevertheless, it would be a relapse to the times of the painted asparagus bundle of Manet, if one were to deny artistic dignity to any subject. A horse, cow or duck do not by nature show anything which would stimulate an artist to set up a monument to them rather than to a clothes-peg, flashlight or pickaxe. On the contrary, four legs (leaving the duck out of consideration) could be most disadvantagous in a representation. Furthermore, it is likely to be more interesting to create a living impression from an inorganic subject.

Let us consider the real reservations. Although we have been talking about an over-sized toothbrush, it is noticeable that the sculpture itself is not over-sized, despite its height of almost six metres. It is very reserved and displays its attractions in a calculated manner in a few exposed places. For example in the narrow edge of the red toothbrush cup, then in the brown tip high up on the blue handle, and finally in the emphasis on the white wavy brush section and the extra curves of the pink paste gently capped at the side. In these places concreteness is noticeable. Volume shows itself, but in the end the colourful geometry always triumphs. This triumph is a gesture which takes place mainly within the framework of the openly structured sculpture. At no point does the sculpture assert itself at the expense of the architecture. From a material point of view the sculpture wishes to exert no influence. However, this does not mean that the outside space is not affected, because it is only since *Cross-section of a Toothbrush* is here, that this space has taken on real form. A light colourful overtone has been added to the serious keynote of the dark brick facade, which, like a locked door, clearly separates the extended street area from the private garden area, making the surrounding area vibrate. The sculpture indeed functions like a tuning-fork here; by touching the hard brick facade it gives off its cheerful-ironic tone all around the space.

But what has happened to the serious reservations that this colourful sculpture is in the wrong place outside? It cannot be ignored that *Cross-section of a Toothbrush* can claim all the freedom of a street sculpture only because it is situated in an architectural space outside. The angular retracted building creates for this visual extract of an idea the appropriate room for a representation which would like to be the subject of a sculpture, but at the same time wants to be untouched, like a thought. There could hardly be another spot in the architectural setting in the town where it could be as effective. Yet, despite all its geometry and discipline, it is too vulnerable to backgrounds and influences. Because of its colourfulness it reacts in an extremely delicate way to all background changes. Unlike other sculptures of Claes Oldenburg, which can easily defy even the highest glass palaces and traffic, it could never stand in the chaos of the streets. *Cross-section of a Toothbrush* needs a secure stage, like the turning circle in front of the Haus Esters. But it returns the favour in its own way, in that it withdraws from the space and allows the house and garden its fitting applause.

A New York architectural critic, learning of the plan to place an Oldenburg sculpture in front of the Haus Esters was heard to remark 'how terrible'. Similar remarks have been made by other critics before the sculpture was in place. It was feared that the Wilhelmshofallee could turn into something like a road approaching Las Vegas. When *Cross-section of a Toothbrush* stood there unveiled, the same critics, who time and again give their judgement before having seen the reality, were disappointed by the smallness of the sculpture. But large and small are not criteria in the evaluation of sculpture, not even in the open space. What is decisive is the appropriateness of the form and that is a question of standards. But precisely these have been lost. And this loss is more painful in respect to town planning than that of the 'golden mean'. We do not need hierarchical or centralistic ideas which prescribe our point of view. We have seen the outcome of this in the Thirties and Forties, from Berlin to Moscow, from Rome to New York. The vital thing is, through individual solutions, to re-relate things square by square, street by street, suburb by suburb so they offer mutual reverence to one another and form new unities in which one element can be understood through the various influences of the other. In this regaining of a transparent urban form from the variety of living fields of activity, art can be of service at various points, optically defining the newly-won territory and giving it new character. No work of art can create new conditions in a defective environment.

The Haus Esters and the *Toothbrush* are a demonstration. They clearly show what matters in the interplay of architecture, art and nature. Even if one can learn little directly from this example on the edge of town so far away from the real problems, the 'concrete Utopia' of this piece, standing clearly before our eyes, strengthens the hope that change is possible.

Adapted from *Claes Oldenburg: Cross Section of a Toothbrush with Paste in a Cup, on a Sink: Portrait of Coosje's Thinking*, Krefelder Kunstmuseen, 1983, pp. 42–63.

Blasted Pencil

Facing page:
Study for a Print of the Blasted Pencil
1983
Felt pen, pencil, crayon
11 × 8½ in (28 × 21.6 cm)

Repression and Resistance
at the University of El Salvador
1968–83

Coosje van Bruggen

An account based on an interview
with Professor José Domínguez[1], published
in *Real Life Magazine*, Number 11–12,
Winter 1983, pp. 15–18, as part of the
Artists Call exhibition held in January 1984
to protest United States intervention in
Central America.

In 1841 the University of El Salvador was founded as an independent institution although financed by the State. However, in 1897, under the national presidency of Rafael Gutierrez, the student newspaper *El Latigo* was forbidden, because it was critical of government policy. The editors were expelled, and the National University was closed. The University reopened again in September 1898 with its autonomy restored, though subsequently the government interfered in its policy on several occasions. In 1939, just before the outbreak of the Second World War, the independence of the University was once again violated when the national president General Maximiliano Hernández Martínez appointed a member of his government to the Rectorship of the University in order to serve his interests. A further analysis of the history of the National University up to the present shows a pattern of government interference in its affairs, alternating with control of the University by progressive students and professors. Each time, the gains of the progressives were suppressed by violent occupation of the campus.

In the 1960s a strong movement towards democratization arose parallel to similar developments at universities in the United States and Europe. A conviction had grown among professors and students that their educational institution belonged to the people and should be accessible to all classes. The University of El Salvador took an independent radical direction which became gradually more and more incongruent with the conservative ideas of the established authorities. Eventually the State of El Salvador and its University became involved in a bitter conflict which continues to the present day.

The large Faculty of Science and Humanities and the smaller Faculties of Economics and Law, all especially aware of the social problems of the country and actively involved in bettering conditions, were the principal progressive force within the University. The hierarchic structure was to be broken down gradually. Directorial decisions in each Faculty were to be made by an equal representation of professors, students and members of professional associations, composed of physicians, lawyers, etc., practicing in El Salvador. In this unique concept of co-government, administrative work was handled by students as well as professors. This inseparability of tasks placed the administration in the service of the academic process instead of the reverse, which occurs in so many overly bureaucratic institutions. Furthermore, students with economic problems were provided with free housing, free use of libraries, and special grants enabling them to acquire books and laboratory equipment needed to enter Faculties such as Medicine or Dentistry.

The equal participation of students in formulating the policy of the University was strongly opposed by the professional associations, whose members belonged mainly to the upper middle-class. At the end of 1970 the collaboration between progressive professors and students culminated in the election of Dr Rafael Menjivar, an advocate of co-government, as Rector of the University. As might be expected, the selection of Dr Menjivar was rejected by the professionals and the conservative professors. They addressed themselves to the General Assembly of El Salvador in an attempt to nullify the election. Although the Rector was elected, the situation was very tense and the controversy over the appointment raised by the federation of professional associations continued.

*Elevations and Patterns
for the Blasted Pencil*
1985
Pencil
43 × 27½ in (109.2 × 69.9 cm)
Drawn by J. Robert Jennings

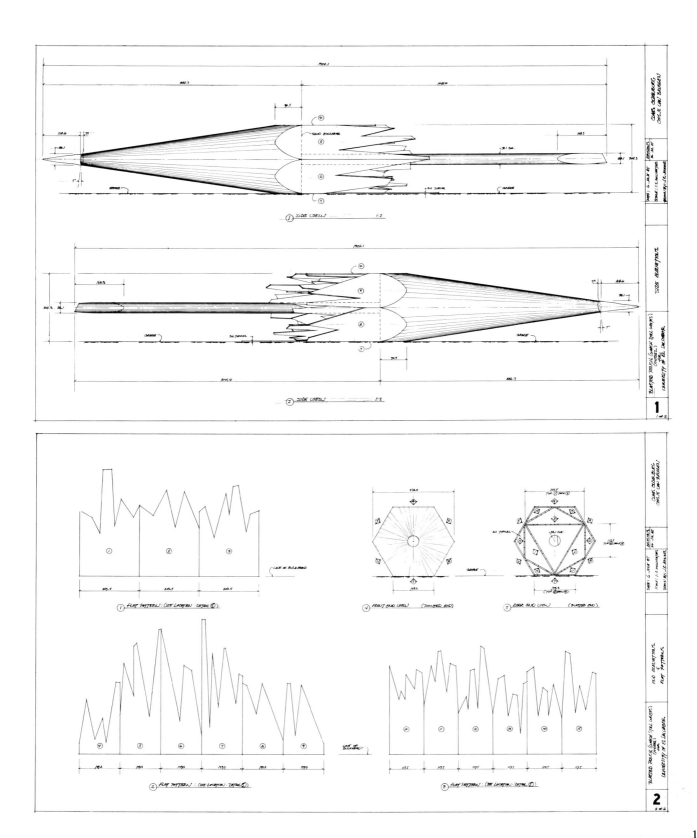

Broken Pencil, Writing
1983
Felt pen, ball-point pen
crayon, watercolour
12 × 8½ in (30.3 × 22 cm)

The tool of communication is damaged but
not out of commission. The will to continue
is transferred with such force to the object
that it starts to act on its own.

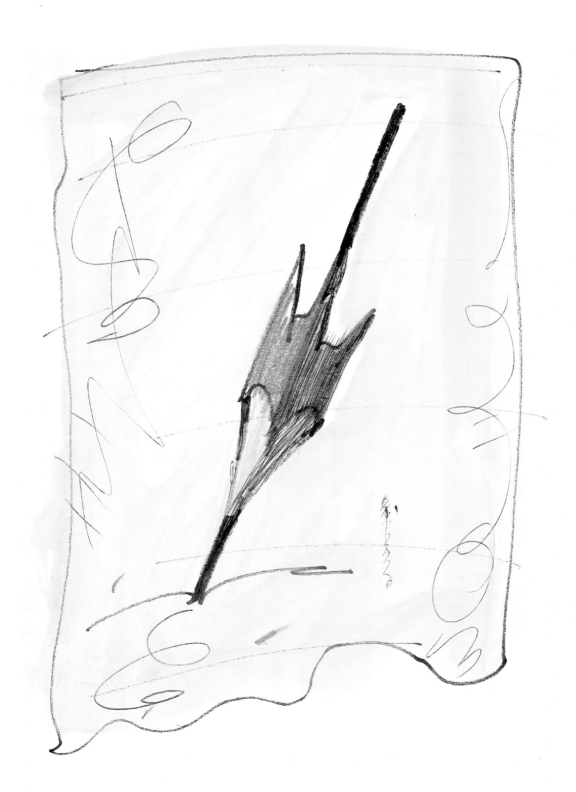

1983

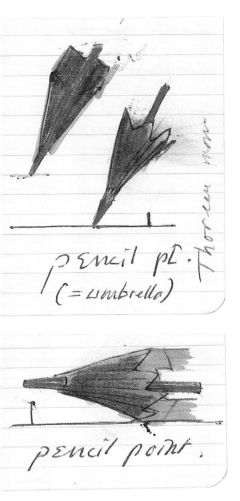

Notebook Page: Pencil Points
1982
Pencil, ball point pen, felt pen
Two sheets 2 × 2¾ in (5 × 7 cm);
3¾ × 2¾ in (9.5 × 7 cm)
On sheet 11 × 8½ in (28 × 21.6 cm)
Because Henry David Thoreau was a pencil-maker, a monument to him might take the shape of a huge broken cylinder of graphite, pointed at one end, to be placed obscurely in a wood, where it could be discovered by a wanderer. Whether it was manufactured by someone or a marvelous chance product of Nature should be a matter for speculation.

During the period of democratization the University played an important role by organizing town meetings in small and large towns in support of the union ANDES (the National Association of Salvadorean Educators), which demanded better salaries for grammar and high-school teachers, and medical aid, pension plans, and reimbursement of salaries suspended by the government during strikes. As a consequence, the government began to harrass teachers and academics who assisted ANDES. This has continued with increasing brutality up to the present time. Amnesty International stated in its report to the U.S. House of Representatives, 26 July 1983:
'The arbitrary arrests, torture, 'disappearances', and extra-judicial executions which have been carried out against them by the regular police and military forces, or the paramilitary groups to which they are linked, appeared to be an attempt to eradicate the union ANDES … ANDES is an active member of the *Bloque Popular Revolucionario* (BRP), the Popular Revolutionary Bloc, which, in turn, is a member of the Revolutionary Democratic Front (FDR)[2]. Teachers may also have been targeted for repression since they are viewed as potential leaders in small communities and, as such, could constitute a focus of opposition to the established authorities.'

The events surrounding the official elections, held in March 1972, show the extent to which the government feared the progressive policy of the University and its close ties to the social conditions in the country. Professor Domínguez states that José Napoleon Duarte, candidate of the Unión Nacional Opositora, a coalition of three parties in the opposition, would have won if the party in power, the PCN (Partido de Conciliación Nacional) had not sabotaged the election by hiring voters and supplying them with several false identification cards. To assure that they themselves would win the elections, the National Guard forcibly removed the ballot boxes in order to stuff them further. As a result an insolent fraud was perpetrated and Colonel Molina was 'officially' elected president.

A large crowd gathered to protest in the Parque Libertad in San Salvador. On the third day of the demonstration the National Guard arrived, capturing hundreds of protestors, many of whom were later killed. The University spoke out in a press conference, stating that the government of Molina was the product of fraud, and would bring repression and injustice.

There were immediate repercussions: seventeen days after Molina became president, government troops occupied the University of El Salvador. José Domínguez describes the situation: 'At the time, we were fighting legally against the federation of professionals who were trying to undo the appointment of Dr Menjivar. On 26 July 1972, while Dr Menjivar and Dr Saénz Varela, the Secretary General of the University, were in the National Palace discussing the issue with the authorities, the General Assembly and the Army had already secretly decided on military intervention. Subsequently, an enormous display of power took place on the campus with guns, tanks, and helicopters. Many students who were attending classes were captured. Dr Rafael Menjivar and Dr Saénz Varela were sent into exile. The University was closed temporarily in order to be reorganized, and put under the control of the federation of professional associations. The pendulum had swung back; the process of radical democratization had been suppressed and the conservative policies of the University were now restored'. In 1973 the University reopened under the control of a 'normalizing' committee, the Comisión

Normalizadora, which dictated rules to the professors, applied disciplinary laws to the students, appointed a University Police, and had the power to expel students and professors without any reason. Students were dismissed from all levels of direction of the University. Because the professors with political affiliations were replaced by others who were sympathetic to the new regime but academically unqualified, the scientific level of the University rapidly decreased.

After a year, progressive professors and students slowly recouped some of their power, because, in order to function, the University was forced to rehire some of the certified professors who had been fired, though at the lower level of instructor. Instructors, most of whom were recent graduates, became the foundation of renewed resistance, sharing the ideas of the students assigned to them. They became minority members in the Councils of the Faculties which also included highly conservative professors and professionals. The threat of job loss diminished among the professors, because the Councils needed unanimity in order to fire people, and never achieved it. Since the people appointed in various Departments in the name of the professional associations were not qualified to teach, the former professors were able to start teaching their courses the way they wanted, slowly repoliticizing the campus.

At the end of 1974 the Faculty of Science and Humanities were openly opposing the Rector of the University, Dr Carlos Alfaro Castillo, because he tried to remove its progressive Dean in order to acquire control over the Faculty. In January of 1975, when the professors needed to get reconfirmation of their appointments, he attempted to fire about thirty of them including the Heads of the Departments of Mathematics and Biology. His plan failed but when the professors went on strike in protest Dr Castillo was able to suspend salaries for three months.

As the conflicts increased and the resistance hardened, the campus police began to display guns, and the National Guard made incursions in the Santa Ana and San Miguel campuses. On 18 July they entered the Santa Ana campus, shot and wounded students, and captured three persons. The next day the students of the National University marched in protest along University Avenue in San Salvador. In front of the Social Security Building a massacre took place. The National Guard was responsible for this convulsive act. About fifty students were killed; many people lying wounded on the street were thrown into trucks and taken away, never to be seen again. On the campus a crowd attacked the police headquarters. Unarmed, the students threw stones, branches and anything they were able to find. The demonstrators were routed by the National Guard. That night the police closed off the University campus, and destroyed all the offices of the student unions.

In November 1976 there was another clash between students and the University Police, when the students organized a protest march inside the campus to accuse Dr Castillo of collaborating with the government in the massacre of 1975, and of continuous repression of progressive students and professors. As a result, on 19 November the University was closed for six months. During that time a new Council was set up by the Legislative Assembly, the Asamblea Legislativa, called the CAPUES, Consejo de Administración Provisional Universidad El Salvador. In May 1977 the University reopened, and was placed entirely under the rule of the Rector, the

Deans of each Faculty, a General Secretary and a fiscal official. The Superior Council and the General University Assembly were dissolved. All the power was put into the hands of the Rector and an oligarchy. Professor Domínguez describes the campus at that time: 'The five entrances of the University were turned into bunkers, and fully armed guards occupied the entrances. Every student and professor needed a permit to get in. In the building where we have the medical offices and counselling services for the students, the CAPUES posted the Police, and made a jail for students, who were occasionally punished and tortured inside.'

However, the state of mind of the progressive students and professors in 1977 was completely different from that of 1972. Many of the professors, and even some members of the professional associations who earlier had not taken a political stand, had become more socially aware due to their experience of injustice and terror at the University. Now they were determined to make sacrifices, to write, and speak out.

In the beginning of 1978 Dr Castillo was murdered. The assassin was never identified. According to rumours at the time, he was either killed by a university policeman, or a member of the Popular Revolutionary Bloc. Castillo was replaced by an engineer, Dr Efraím Jovel, formerly Dean of the Faculty of Agronomical Sciences, who continued the CAPUES. In September 1978 the CAPUES aroused violent opposition in the Faculty of Science and Humanities by replacing its Dean with the conservative professor Dr Paredes, who had been dismissed in 1970 by the students. A 'coordinating' committee of progressive students and professors was formed to solve the dispute. The response was the firing of fifty professors and instructors, but the opposition to the Dean continued, and made it impossible for him to function. At the same time the students in the Faculty of Economics demonstrated against the CAPUES. Its Dean, Dr Rodriguez, who went to the Council to discuss the grievances, was murdered by the University Police. The opposition of the Faculty of Science and Humanities then intensified to such an extent that the CAPUES closed them down. Professor Domínguez states: 'We went to the press, radio and television to say that despite this we would continue to function. We would have classes, tests, examinations, everything.' The Faculty of Economics reacted differently. They closed down in protest against the assassination of the Dean, and entered into discussions with the professional associations to obtain their support.

On 17 December 1978 the National Assembly in El Salvador gave in to the opposition. It was impossible for it to support the CAPUES morally or legally any longer in view of the evidence presented in the newspapers of the kidnapping, torture and assassination of students and professors by the University Pòlice. A provisional Council, the Consejo Directivo Provisional, consisting only of professors, was formed on 27 December to draw up a new legal code for the University, which was respected for a year and a half.

The government of General Romero had succeeded that of Colonel Molina in 1977. Romero's government was overthrown in 1979. The ruling juntas which followed only worsened the situation. On 26 June 1980 the National Guard suddenly occupied the campus again, this time without any provocation by students or professors. The first pretext given was that a military patrol had been shot at from the University. Then the story was changed; it was said that the Guard was looking for weapons. The military claimed that corpses used for scientific purposes in the Faculty of Medicine were those of people kidnapped by guerillas using the sewer system to enter and leave the campus. The University was pillaged by the soldiers. Laboratory equipment was destroyed, and the Library of Social Sciences was set on fire, ostensibly because it was contaminated with foreign ideologies such as communism.

Amnesty International has repeatedly appealed to the authorities to investigate and account for the arbitrary detentions and thousands of cases of 'disappearances' and probable murders:

Fluvio Soriano, professor, Faculty of Agronomical Sciences. Kidnapped 26 May 1979; killed.

José María Portillo Montenegro, professor, Faculty of Agronomical Sciences. Killed July 1979.

Armando Sibrián, professor, Faculty of Science and Humanities, Department of Psychology. Killed December 1979.

Mirna Ochoa de Vásquez, professor, Faculty of Science and Humanities, Department of Psychology. Killed December 1979.

María Teresa Cevallos, professor, Faculty of Science and Humanities, Department of Sociology. Killed 1979.

María Magdalena Henríquez, student, Faculty of Pharmacology and member of the commission of human rights. Kidnapped 3 October 1980; her body was found 7 October 1980.

Félix Antonio Ullóa, Rector of the National University. Killed October 1980.

Enrique Escobar Barrera, student and instructor, Faculty of Science and Humanities; member of the MNR and of the Directory of the FDR. Killed 27 November 1980.

Manuel de Jesús Franco, professor, Faculty of Economics; member of the Directory of the FDR and the Nationalist Democratic Union. Killed 27 November 1980.

Humberto Mendoza, student; member of the Directory of the FDR and The United Peoples' Action Front. Killed 27 November 1980.

Douglas Mauricio Ramirez and his wife Rosa Mélida Ramirez, both professors. Disappeared in 1980; presumed dead.

Raúl Beltrán Navarrete, professor. Abducted 14 May 1982; presumed dead.

Hugo Carrillo Cabrera, Faculty of Law. Abducted 14 September 1983; presumed dead.

Pedro Flores Peña, student, Faculty of Law, and member of the Superior Council. Abducted 13 September 1983; found dead 24 September 1983.

Jaime Enríquez Bautista, student. Abducted September 1983; presumed dead.

Carlos Adilio Díaz, student. Abducted September 1983; presumed dead.

Manuel de Jesús Baires, Secretary, Faculty of Engineering. Killed September 1983.

Dora Muñóz Castillo, professor, Faculty of Chemistry and Pharmacology. Killed October 1983.

Tortures, assassinations, 'disappearances' of students, professors or members of their families continue. To be part of the University is considered a crime. Nevertheless, at this moment the University of El Salvador continues to function outside the physical campus. All Faculties are operating; classes are being taught at almost all graduate levels. The Rector, Dr Miguel Angel Parada, said at a press conference, held in New York in October 1983: 'The University, in direct confrontation and opposition to dictatorship, is a refugee centre and source of ideas, and therefore has to exclude all totalitarian ideas.' He explained that in 1981 the University received 50% of the budget of 1980, in 1982 50% of the budget of 1981, and in 1983 50% of the budget of 1982! Despite this the University has been able to function, and the number of students has increased to 16,000, providing the substance of the University's continued existence.

Asked if the University is a member of the Revolutionary Democratic Front Dr Parada answered: 'By law no University can be affiliated with one party. We support the FDR's stands, as an observer who can guide it, give it a more rational and measured type of policy. In an orchestra every musician has a different instrument to play. If they play it correctly, the music will sound right, but if you ask them to play the wrong instrument it will sound wrong. The University plays an instrument that nobody else in El Salvador plays.'

The government of El Salvador subjects prisoners to inhuman punishment, tolerates political assassinations, and crushes the centre of its culture, the National University. That the Reagan administration gives military and economic support to this government despite the commitment of the United States to international human rights laws, is a burning injustice. Meanwhile, the heroic struggle for survival of the University of El Salvador goes on.

Postscript by Coosje van Bruggen, 1987

From 1984 up to the present, Amnesty International has continued to receive reports of human rights violations. Specifically the plight of trade unionists, university staff and students, who are suspected of being in opposition to the government, has not changed, as a sampling of case histories from the University of El Salvador demonstrates:

On 19 July 1985, Amnesty International sent a telex to President José Napoléon Duarte expressing its serious concern over reports that eleven professors and students of the University of El Salvador (U.E.S.) were named on a death threat list issued on 12 July in the name of Ejército Secreto Anticommunista (E.S.A.), Secret Anti-Communist Army, a right-wing, para-military death squad.

On 7 March 1986, Morena Margarita Rivas Quijada, age 25, language student and secretary, was taken into custody in San Salvador, while on her way from work, by Members of the Policía de Hacienda (Treasury Police). At the time, she was three months pregnant.

On 7 May 1986, shots were fired at the office of the Dean of the Economics Faculty, Lic. Carlos Henríquez during a meeting of the Faculty board. In an anonymous telephone call, Lic. Carlos Henríquez is said to have been threatened with death unless he left the country within the next three days. Moreover, University officials have reportedly been informed that a plan exists to kill Ing. Manuel Cañas Lazo, Dean of the Engineering Faculty, and Lic. Adán Mejía, Dean of the Law Faculty.

Proposal for a Monument to the Survival of the University of El Salvador: Blasted Pencil (Which Still Writes), Model
1983
Cardboard, urethane foam, wood metal, painted
11 × 84 × 24 in (28 × 213.4 × 61 cm)
Collection Beijer, Stockholm

The *Blasted Pencil Model*, after being shown in the Artists Call exhibition at the Judson Memorial Church in New York, was donated, along with the engineering plans for a large-scale version, to the University of El Salvador.

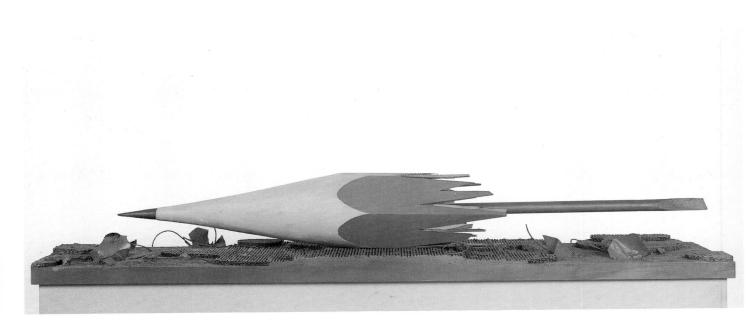

On 19 May 1986, Amnesty International received reports that a grenade was placed in the house of Dra. Ana Gloria Castañeda, the University Secretary General, and that the room in which her children were sleeping was riddled with bullets. Just before the incident, Dra. Castañeda had received a telephone call warning her that she would be killed unless she left the country within the next twenty-four hours.

On 20 May 1986, the student Rufino Antonio Quezada, President of the Associación General de Estudiantes Universitarios Salvadoreños (A.G.E.U.S.), whose name had been included on the E.S.A. death threat list, was detained in San Salvador by members of the National Police and released four days later. Quezada, who subsequently left the country, said, as reported by U.P.I., 'I don't belong to the guerrillas or to a political party. I'm a student leader.'

Death threats have also been received by A.G.E.U.S. representative, Julio Sosa, a psychology student, who had recently returned from the United States.

On 27 April 1987, Professor Antonio Menjivar Flores of the Economics Faculty was assassinated at the University, following the deaths of three members of the National Guard on 12 August near the campus. Condemning the act of violence, A.G.E.U.S. stated: 'These actions by the security forces . . . are to silence the voice of the university which is demanding from the Duarte government respect for its community and a fair budget.'

President Duarte, who was elected with the backing of the United States government, promised in his inaugural speech on 1 June 1984, to 'fight openly and tirelessly to control abuse of authority and the violence of the extremes, the death squads and all the problems of injustice and power they represent'. However, in most human rights violations since then, the perpetrators have remained immune to genuine investigations and prosecution; they have not been held accountable for their acts.

As long as justice is denied and violence against groups of civilians is daily practice, the suffering of professors and students of the University of El Salvador will continue. The *Blasted Pencil (Which Still Writes)* is a monument to their courage and to their determination to keep the University of El Salvador functioning in spite of the policy of terror.

1. José Domínguez was professor in Philosophy from 1968 until 1981 at the National University. In 1980 he became a member of the Superior Council. In January 1981, under threat to his life, he left the country and now lives in the United States, working as a sexton in a Lutheran church. Professor Domínguez is a member of INALSE, The Institute for the Arts and Letters of El Salvador in Exile. The conversations on which this account of the history of the University is based were held in October 1983.

2. The FDR, founded 2 April 1980, is a political coalition of about 35 organizations including opposition parties such as MNR (the socialist movement), labour unions, professional unions and mass organizations.

= eraser
positions

Douse the Glim

Facing page:
Notebook Page: Paper Match Variations
1987
Pencil, felt pen
ball-point pen, crayon
$11 \times 8\frac{1}{2}$ in (28×21.6 cm)
By having the matches torn off in different
configurations, the *Match Cover* sculpture
can spread out over a larger area, away from
a monolithic conception.

*Study for a Sculpture in the Form
of a Lighted Match in Wind*
1986
Foam-core, paper, wood, spray enamel
12 × 5 × 3¾ in (30.5 × 12.7 × 9.5 cm)

An early, unsubmitted proposal for the
town of Middlesbrough in England,
suggested by a night photo of flaming
refinery chimneys. This proposal makes a
positive, lyrical emblem, like a flag, but one
we found too sentimental, without any
ingredient of contradiction.

*Studies for Sculptures in the Form
of a Snapped Match*
1982
Wood, paper, clay
4⅞ × 5⅝ × 4⅜ in
(12.4 × 14.3 × 3.4 cm)

You are supposed to break matches when
camping out, so as not to start forest fires.
Different ways of doing this, in different
scales and with match-heads of different
colours, make a group for a small square in
an unsubmitted proposal for the town of
Vail, Colorado, in the Rocky Mountains.

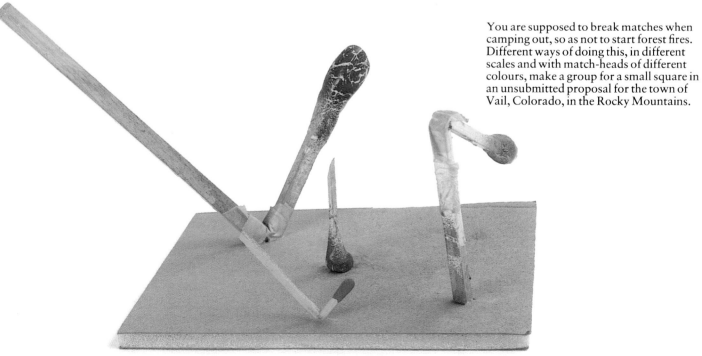

Match Cover
1961
Plaster on burlap, enamel
3$^{15}/_{16}$ × 2$^{3}/_{4}$ × 1$^{3}/_{16}$ in
(10 × 7 × 3 cm)

The *Match Cover* is an object in the
inventory of *The Store*, 1961. Like a
lowered curtain, the cover is nearly closed.
The matches inside are not allowed to exert
themselves; they must be imagined.
Painting predominates; what is important is
the equivalence between the cover and
a canvas.

*Study for a Sculpture in the Form
of a Match Cover*
1987
Wood, paper, clay; latex
7 × 6$^{1}/_{2}$ × 4$^{1}/_{2}$ in
(17.8 × 16.5 × 11.4 cm)
set in base 1$^{1}/_{4}$ × 10$^{1}/_{2}$ × 9 in
(3.2 × 26.7 × 22.9 cm)

The sculptural potential of a match cover
is released in a spontaneous, rapidly executed
sketch, which recalls the many-armed figures
in Indian sculpture. At this moment, the
match subject moves from the single match,
where it has stayed since 1979, to a 'cluster',
which makes it complex enough to serve as a
large-scale project.

Notebook Page: Studies Towards
a Sculpture for Barcelona
1987
Pencil, coloured pencil, felt pen
Two sheets 2¾ × 5 in (7 × 12.7 cm)
detail from sheet 11 × 8½ in
(28 × 21.6 cm)

We have received a commission in Barcelona, for one of the city parks being developed there as part of the attempt by the Socialist government to reestablish the artistic prominence of the city after the many years of neglect under Franco's regime. I have brought back the usual collection of guides, brochures, history books, snapshots and personal impressions, in search of some indigenous visual stereotypes that can be intertwined with our subjects to arrive at the proposal. In these sketches I invoke Flamencan dance shoes and fans, mixing them with Piccassoid visages and ferocious streetcars (Gaudí was killed by one). The drama takes place on a field which may be a bull ring or the famous surrealist plane where the umbrella encounters the sewing machine.

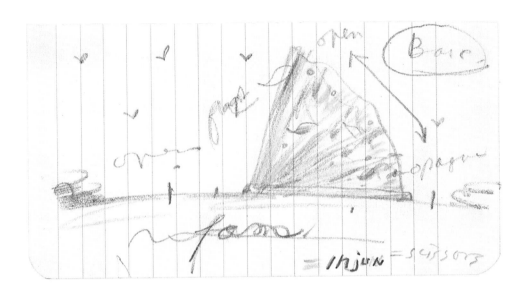

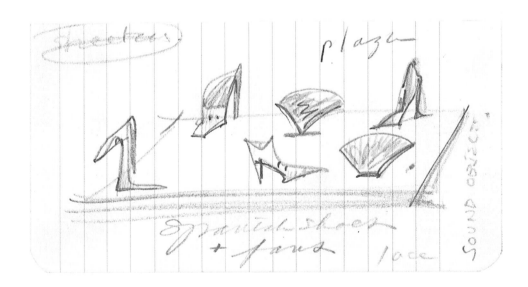

180

*Sculpture in the Form of a Match Cover
Fabrication Study*
1987
Cardboard, expanded polyurethane
40½ × 24⅜ × 18 in
(102.9 × 61.9 × 45.7 cm)

Copy of the Chicago Picasso Maquette
1969
Cardboard, wood
40 × 24⅜ × 29½ in
(101.6 × 61.9 × 74.9 cm)

In 1969, I made a copy in cardboard of the
maquette for the Chicago Picasso, as a step to
realizing a soft version (now in the collection
of the Musée nationale d'art moderne,
Centre Georges Pompidou, Paris). I had been
commissioned to make the copy by William
Copley, the painter, who wanted it known
that Picasso had given free use of the image
to the people of Chicago and the city had
no right to restrict it. After building the
large *Match Cover Model*, also in cardboard,
I realised its similarities to the Picasso
maquette. I went down to the basement of
Broome Street and recovered the battered
and dusty copy for comparison. Quite
differently from our procedure, Picasso had
ignored all the possible inspirations related to
the site brought to him by his admirers in
Chicago who wished to commission a large
outdoor sculpture. The inspirations included
an Indian headdress and a baseball catcher's
uniform. The Chicago Picasso has always
seemed to me to have a portable quality
despite its size, like the souvenirs of it sold by
the city: my favourite is a pair of cufflinks.

181

Stirring Up Spanish Themes
1987
Pencil, watercolour, felt pen
30⅛ × 23¼ in (76.5 × 59 cm)
Inscription by Coosje van Bruggen

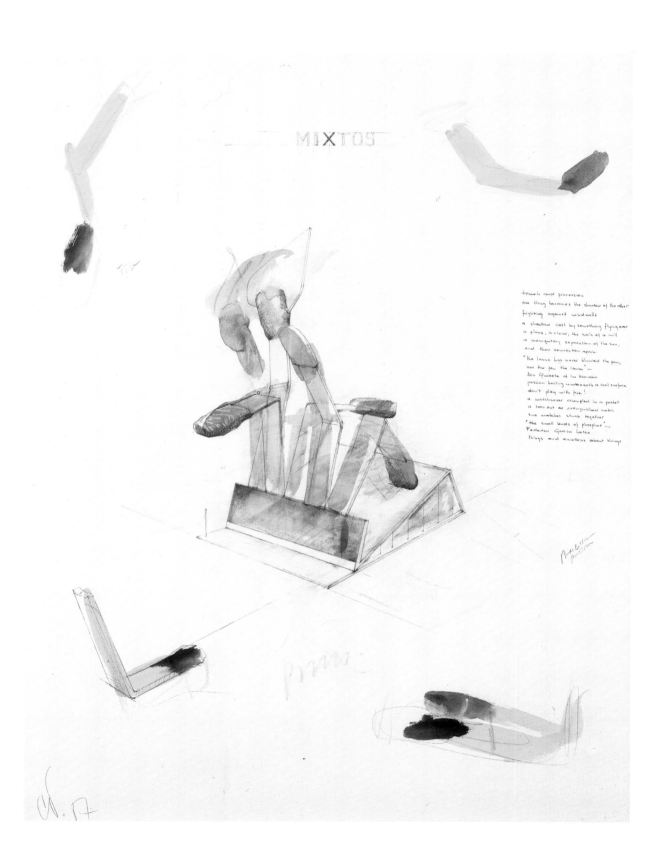

At this point, the sculpture has not been engineered and the weight, cost, and even the practicability of the work is unknown. Nevertheless, we agree that the *Match Cover*, with scattered matches, should become our first suggestion for the commission in Barcelona. The 'matches' will be steel and the 'heads' could be of ceramic. Barcelona is known for both, and one reason the subject seemed right is that it offered the opportunity to combine these two materials. Early matches tended to be red. The colours would be strong and primary, together with intense black. An image could be developed for the 'cover' and the base might be a building. The *Match Cover* represents different destinies of the same form. The arrangement of matches in a cover suggests a crowd, which is gradually decimated. One can also speak of a parade, with flags or placards. The matches might be compared to the Pillars of Hercules. By coincidence, the sculpture echoes the shape of the Sagrada Familia by Gaudí. If the *Match Cover* were to be approximately the same height as the Chicago Picasso, each match would be 42 inches wide and four inches thick.

trench and procession
one thing becomes the shadow of the other
fighting against windmills
a shadow cast by something flying over
a plane, a cloud, the sails of a mill
a momentary separation of the sun,
and then connection again.
"the lance has never blunted the pen,
  nor the pen the lance" —
  Don Quixote of La Mancha
  passion boiling underneath a cool surface
  don't play with fire!
  a matchcover crumpled in a pocket
  a torn out or extinguished match
  two matches stuck together
"the small buds of phosphor" —
Federico Garcia Lorca
  things and emotions about things

Sculpture in the Form of a Match Cover
Fabrication Model
1987
Steel, expanded polyurethane
epoxy; latex
40 × 26 × 18 in
(101.6 × 66 × 45.7 cm)

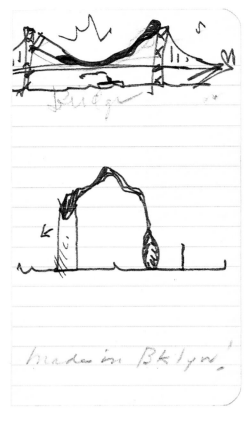

The large version of the *Extinguished
Match* was carved in a loft on the Brooklyn
side of the East River. The trip was always
across, and through the arches of the
Brooklyn Bridge.

xtinguished Match
987
teel, urethane foam; latex
ft 10 in × 22 ft 6 in × 29 in
238.8 × 685.8 × 73.7 cm)

After trying several positions of the single *Match*, the unaided one, just laying on the ground, seemed the best. The curve which occurs during combustion is exaggerated in order to lift up the ends, which are sharply contrasted: black and white; organic and geometric, etc. The sculpture has been given a specific interpretation in two instances, by the inclusion of its prototype in 'Disarming Images', an exhibition against nuclear armament, 1984–85, and in a benefit exhibition for the American Foundation for AIDS Research, in 1987.

The Haunted House

Facing page:
Haunted House (original for poster)
1987
Charcoal, chalk, pastel on paper
40 × 30 in (101.6 × 76.2 cm)

Ghosting

Coosje van Bruggen

On top of a hill behind which the sun begins to set, a solitary mansion is silhouetted against the scarlet sky. It seems in a ruined state; most of the windows are shattered or boarded up. Apparently the house has been uninhabited for quite some time, and it might even be haunted, for at night, so the story goes, bright lights emanate from its interior. The dream image is suddenly completed by a flash of lightning, which jars the memory, and the scene shifts to a swanky allee in a city in Nordrhein-Westfalen, on the edge of the Ruhr district, focusing on a villa surrounded by a well-groomed old garden. A brick house dating from the 1920s, it stands in a specific architectural relationship to the neighbouring villa: weren't the two designed for the families of Hermann Lange and Josef Esters, managing directors of the United Silk Weaving Mills in Krefeld? The scrap of memory stimulates a more recent image of the same villas, each with its own scheme of free-flowing, open interior spaces lit by conspicuous bands of windows. But now the Haus Esters seems curiously uninhabited: its rooms, all painted white, are nearly empty. Here and there strange, colourful objects stand on the floor, hang on the walls, or sit on pedestals. In a corner of the entrance hall lies a dilapidated version of a folding chair seen earlier in the house. (Does it have some connection to Barcelona?)

At first the hackneyed image of the decrepit haunted house on the hill seems to evoke no analogies with the carefully tended villas, now turned into museums, so inherently opposed to triviality. But what happens at night? Their shutters are still lowered to keep out burglars. Is this just a left-over custom, a reminder of their original function as a place to live in? 'We are all haunted houses,' the poet H.D. wrote in her *Tribute to Freud*. We are haunted by our past, lived in by ghosts, stand-ins for those we fear. The associations that arise in our dreams stimulate not only the memory but also the imagination, and it is precisely here that the artist makes his entrance. In *The Haunted House*, through his decision to transform the prominent band of windows of Haus Esters, Claes Oldenburg simultaneously alters its exterior and its interior appearance at the same time as he touches on a deep vulnerability in community life. People are proud to show off their homes through their impeccably clean bay windows, yet they fear burglary. Here, of necessity, functional issues dominated the vision of the architect of Haus Esters, Mies van der Rohe. And here the artist asserts himself through the creation of substitute windows, 'ghost' windows which are of no practical use at all. Their 'glass' is shattered; as it no longer insulates the inside from the outside world, the imagination and its anxieties are all let loose.

The equivalence between a window and a painting, both rectangular planes supported by a frame, allows Oldenburg to play on the interaction between Haus Esters' roles as a home and as a museum, and on the interaction between art, architecture, and life.

To merge these different areas some of the 'broken windows' have been taken out; they lean against the wall like paintings still to be hung or rejects waiting for a substitute. The visitor to the house might get the impression that the show is not yet mounted or already in the stage of being taken down. The artist's substitute windows consist of triple-ply cardboard sheets cut to fill the existing openings in the walls. They are fastened to heavy-duty stretchers that are invisible from the inside of the house and that from the outside remind one of the backs of scenery flats.

The Haunted House
1987
Installation at Museum Haus Esters
Krefeld, 1987

Geometric Mouse Banners
1969
Nylon
Each 138 × 77 in
(350.5 × 195.6 cm)
Installed in front of the
Museum of Modern Art
New York 1969

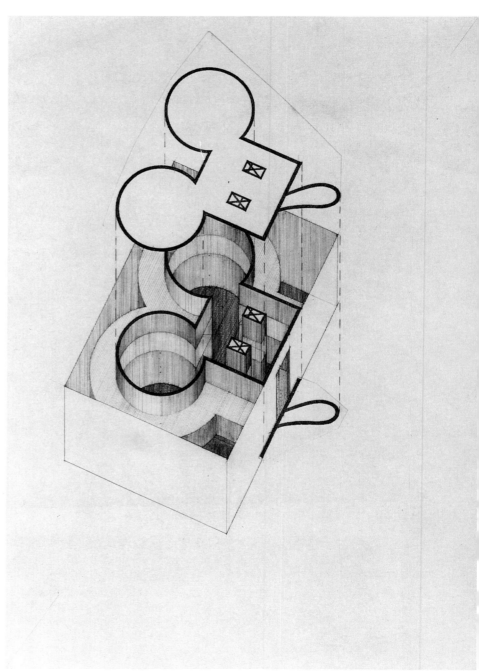

Plan for a Small Museum in the Shape
of a Geometric Mouse
1972
Rubber stamp, pencil, collage
13½ × 11 in (34.5 × 28 cm)

Mouse Museum and *Ray Gun Wing*
1972–77
Detail of the interior of the *Mouse Museum*
Ludwig Collection, Vienna

Detail of *Tools of the Trade*
1982
Aluminum, masonite, wood; latex
Installed in the Fridericianum, Kassel
during Documenta 7, 1982

These 'broken windows' are enlarged from carefully drawn plans on the windows of a small scale model that Oldenburg made of the house. Each window has a different composition: its rectangular form is traversed by radiuses and straight lines in combinations arrived at intuitively yet which are firmly geometric. Most of the resulting divisions stay attached to the frame, but the ones in the centre are cut out and tilted, dropped in the window well or on the floor. These shards are realized in a scale much larger than normal glass splinters; once they have left the rectangle of the 'broken window,' they lose their identity. Depending on their position and size, they can become anything from a painting to some bit of debris, from sculpture to obstacle.

In contrast to the rigidity of the patterns that divide the window fragments, the diagonal paths of white, grey, and black paint that cover them move freely across their surfaces. To avoid a naturalistic appearance, their application is based on graphic representations of windows such as those in comic strips. Starting one step away from the real, Oldenburg creates variations not so much on broken windows themselves as on the sign for them. This sign, in its simplicity, lends itself well to a sculptural presentation. In making an object in the form of a flat picture and intensifying its three-dimensionality by using an obviously tangible material, cardboard, and by actually breaking up its surface, the artist not only shifts between painting and sculpture but also sets up an ambiguity between reality and imagination. The cardboard, illusionistically painted to appear as shiny as glass, becomes an intermediate material between glass and canvas. It's true that in comparison to the existing window, the stand-in placed in front of it may seem a grimace, a distortion of the real; it may suggest the boarded-up house of the horror movie. However, in their carefully laid-out geometric schemes, and in their application of paint which stylistically recalls fundamental painting, these windows are no longer merely a film set mimicking reality; they are alienated into art.

When we were talking about these broken windows, seemingly shattered by objects thrown through them, Oldenburg remarked:
'The theme of all things that I've done in the area of installation, starting with The *Tools of The Trade* for Documenta 7 in 1982, has involved the forcible penetration of the museum, in some way the representation of the coming into the museum of the outside, or the intrusion of the objective world into the subjective world and the combination of the two inside the museum. But it's not as aggressive a statement as it appears. It's more the idea that the objects should be halfway outside and halfway inside, a variation on the attempt to bring art and life together. And that's the function that windows might also serve: they are the gate between subjectivity and objectivity, being the way that the brain perceives the outside world, and the way that the outside world enters the brain.

In the *Geometric Mouse* the 'eyes' have shutters, the object resembles a camera. The 'eyes' in the *Geometric Mouse Banners* are Xed, like the sign for unconsciousness in comic strips or the diagonal taping done on windows in newly erected skyscrapers. The *Mouse Museum* identifies the head with a house (mouse equals house). Its contents are the memory, and the 'eyes' become plastic cases filled with objects. When the 'eyes' or the windows are broken, the outside enters more quickly, like the house sinking with the dead father in *Huckleberry Finn*'.[1]

Soft Air Flow, Model 2
(Front End)
1965
Canvas, kapok; spray enamel
42¼ × 25¾ × 13 in
(107.3 × 65.4 × 33 cm)
Collection William J. Hokin
Chicago

Model (Ghost) Typewriter
1963
Canvas, kapok, wood
27½ × 26 × 9 in (69.8 × 66 × 22.9 cm)
Museum für Moderne Kunst
Frankfurt am Main

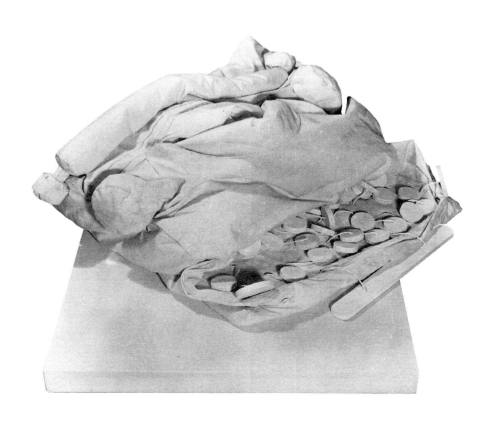

Empire Papa Ray Gun
1959
Newspaper, wheat paste
wire; casein
40¾ × 39¼ × 13½ in
(103.5 × 99.7 × 34.3 cm)
Museum of Modern Art
New York

As one approaches Haus Esters, then, what at first sight may appear an act of vandalism toward the architecture on the part of the artist, the throwing of objects through the windows of the main floor, may eventually be seen as a creative act tying together painting and sculpture, juxtaposing two parallel realities: the imaginary one of the artist and the functional one of the architect.

In any case, the aggression signified by the broken windows is offset by the materials used. You can't cut yourself on glass splinters made of cardboard; the sting is taken out, just as it is with Oldenburg's *Ray Gun* from the early 60's, which 'illuminates but doesn't kill,' and as it is with the softened *Airflow* automobile from 1965, which denies the violent potential of crushed metal. Similarly, a brick that seems to have been thrown through the windows is made out of styrofoam. It is a 'wimpy' brick. Lightly floating through space, hitting the window, it would probably bounce back. Thrown in one's face, it wouldn't hurt any more than a cake.

The release of violence is transformed into an energizing force, as it is in George Herriman's *Krazy Kat* comic strip when Ignatz the mouse throws his bricks at the Kat, who loves being hit. When the brick bounces off Krazy Kat's head, a little heart spirals off from it as well, symbolizing her gratitude to the mouse for paying her attention. Oldenburg prefers Ignatz, who in his ingenious wickedness is described as 'a malignant little tangle of barbed wire,' to the welladjusted, conformist Mickey Mouse. Though Mickey started as a poor mouse in Kansas City, he became a rather bourgeois mouse in Hollywood, whereas Ignatz always stayed an outlaw mouse. And Oldenburg too throws brickbats, aimed at the museum, although, in a mixed reaction of respect and contempt, he also throws bouquets. He has remained consistent with his 'I am for' statements from the 1960s, as a small selection of them may show:

'I am for an art that is political-erotical-mystical, that does something other than sits on its ass in a museum . . . I am for an art that embroils itself with the everyday crap and still comes out on top . . . I am for the art of scratchings in the asphalt, daubing at the walls. I am for the art of bending and kicking metal and breaking glass, and pulling at things to make them fall down.'[2]

Model of *The Haunted House*
for Haus Esters
1987
Wood, paper, cloth, etc; latex
4⅛ × 38 × 16¾ in
(10.5 × 96.5 × 42.5 cm)

George Herriman
Krazy Kat
8 September 1940

Models for Objects in the Haunted House
Haus Esters
1986
Paper, expanded polystyrene, cloth; latex
Objects:
Birdhouse 4¾ in (12 cm)
Broken Bottle 2¾ in (7 cm)
Half Tire and Tube 3¼ in (8.3 cm)
Brickbat 2 in (5 cm)
Muffler 5½ in (14 cm)
Log 2⅞ in (7.3 cm)

Notebook Page: Studies for the Haunted House: Bricks, Broken Record etc
March 1987
Felt pen
8¹¹/₁₆ × 6 in (22 × 15.2 cm) detail from
sheet 11 × 8½ in (28 × 21.6 cm)

The *Half Tire* is probably the result
of the chance juxtaposition of
a broken record and a discarded tyre in
the lot behind our building in New York.

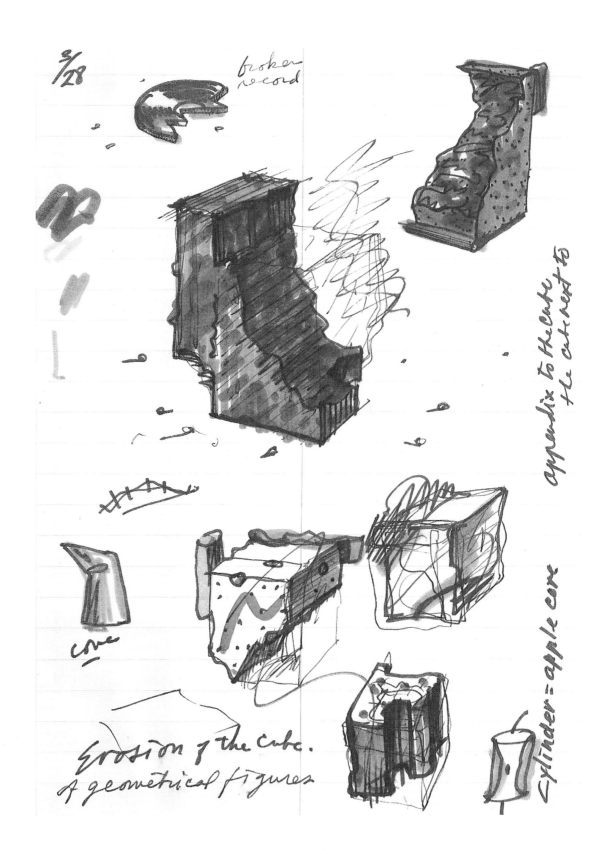

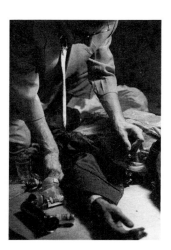

World's Fair II at *The Store*
New York, 1962
Performer extracts belongings
from the suit of the corpse

Ink Bottle
1956
Ink
11 × 8½ in
(28 × 21.6 cm)

Arriving at the Wilhelmshofallee, one discovers that the artist has done his damage and then, as usual, disappeared:

'No one knows where he went. He leaves his signs here and there. He is seen in this part of town and the next moment, miraculously, on the other side of town. One senses him rather than sees him, a lounger, a drunkard, a tennis-player, a bicycle rider, always violently denying that he did it. Everyone gives a different description of the criminal.'[3]

Clearly something has happened here; the windows are broken, and an assortment of odd objects is dispersed through the house. Are we supposed to become the players in a game of Clue? ('Mr. Boddy, apparently the victim of foul play, is found in one of the rooms in his mansion. To win you must determine the answers to these three questions: 1. Who done it? 2. Where? and 3. How?') Any group of objects placed in a dramatic setting has the potential to disclose clues to its origins. Furthermore, the condition of the objects: cracked, scratched, bent, and so forth, may evoke memories of events they were part of, and even provide the motives for those events. Was the crime committed in the hall with a muffler, or maybe in the dining room with a bottle? We discover that the case is unsolvable; the criminal has erased all truly revealing traces of evidence. There's no way to track down the specific brand of muffler. All we are left with is a flattened general form, like a dead raccoon lying in the road, run over by one car after another. There remains of the bottle only its neck, and a label tied around it is torn so that we can read only the letter N. Another dead end: we will never be able to decipher what the label said, or whether the liquid in the bottle was poisoned. Moreover, the body has never been found. The whole case may just as well be an image in a dream of this writer, who is standing in for the artist in the role of a crime reporter.

We do know, however, that, if it was the artist who left these clues in Haus Esters, he left behind a haunted house, frozen in time, like a Victorian mansion he remembers in Evanston, Illinois, which was preserved precisely as it was at the moment when the bridegroom, coming to take his bride to their wedding, died suddenly on the parlour floor. His car was left in the driveway, and not one piece of furniture or personal belongings was moved for over twenty-five years. What has happened to Haus Esters seems a similarly aimless twist of fate. With the breaking of the windows, and the various other things dropped in, the villa has lost its severe architectural quality. Entropy has set in; it's like spring, when the snow melts, revealing all the debris collected beneath. Yet the mood in the house is autumnal. Remnants of man-made objects, decayed relics of everyday life fallen subject to nature's inevitable corruption, are on permanent display, a Beckettian rubble. They are oversized, as if seen from a child's perspective.

Searching among the debris for durable remains and reminders of a civilization, we find no consistency of time or place. *Half Tire and Deflated Tube*, a white-wall tyre cut in half with a collapsed inner tube hanging out of it, transports us to the 1930s. A remembrance of things past, a symbol of affluence, the car in the driveway of the Evanston home transferred to Haus Esters? The artist points out, 'Back then when you were rich, you bought white-walls, because they conveyed elegance.' In another room, however, lies a clear sign of the present, *Rotten Apple Core*, the residue of a natural form altered by man. It hasn't completely disintegrated yet, so it can't have been

Thomas Cole
The Titan's Goblet
1833
Oil on canvas
19⅜ × 16⅛ in (49.2 × 41 cm)
The Metropolitan Museum of Art
Gift of Samuel Avery, Jr, 1904

*Notebook Page: Apple Core
Derived from a Sphere*
1987
Pencil
11 × 8½ in (28 × 21.6 cm)

thrown away too long ago. The crumpled, timeless *Calico Bunny* with its pitch-black, dangling eyes may have been tossed indifferently into a corner, awaiting the fate of being thrown out of the house to undergo painful adventures like a toy in one of Hans Christian Andersen's fairytales. On the other hand it might just have been saved from the gutter by a sentimental collector. With its overlong ears, a cross between a hare and a rabbit, the bunny's formless, blue-checkered canvas body is contained by a primitive profile derived from a cookie cutter. A relic from the past and thus another ghost, this symbol of the home in the form of a two-dimensional rag doll is an artificial counterpart to the rabbits constantly spotted on the museum grounds. *Broken Bottle with Label Fragment*, in its turn, evokes associations from Aladdin's genie through a parable of disobedience in *Struwwelpeter* to a painting in the Metropolitan Museum of Art, New York, by Thomas Cole, *The Titan's Goblet*, 1833, in which the liquid in the goblet is represented as a lake with full-size sailboats. *Uprooted Birdhouse*, with its four sides, roof,

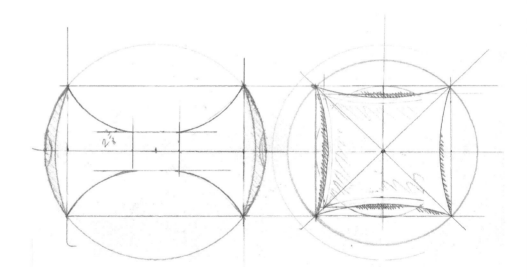

and hole, the most elementary type of house, in its vulnerable position also summons a microcosm of childhood memories: the tilted house in *Huckleberry Finn*, Winnie the Pooh's tree house, the flying house in *The Wizard of Oz*. To Oldenburg, all this is not just a matter of putting suggestive objects together with historical bric-a-brac:
'On analysis, some of the things may reflect the museum and/or home where the exhibition takes place, but the overriding effect should be of blind chance, of objects randomly accumulated in the city.'
As we move from room to room we find no planned narrative, plot, or progression beyond those correspondences that arise spontaneously. Three of the objects, for instance, consist of a body with a single appendage: *Cinder Block and Mortar*, has its reinforcing rod, *Dropped Muffler*, its exhaust pipe, and *Uprooted Birdhouse* its post. All three protuberances are rudely disconnected. Despite the intruding object fragments, each room keeps its sense of intimacy, of someone having been there or lived there.

Rotten Apple Core
1987
Canvas, polyurethane foam
polyurethane resin, steel; latex
65 × 48 × 48 in
(165.1 × 121.92 × 121.92 cm)

Crossection of a Toothbrush with Paste in a
Cup on a Sink: Portrait of Coosje's
Thinking, Soft and Uprooted Version,
with Foundation
1987
Canvas, polyurethane foam; latex.
Foundation: Expanded polystyrene;
Thoroseal, latex, 21 ft × 6¾ × 71⅝ in
(6.4 m × 17.19 × 181.9 cm)
Foundation 36 × 47 × 47 in
(91.44 × 119.38 × 119.38 cm)

Calico Bunny
1987
Canvas, balsawood
expanded polystyrene; latex
72 × 45 × 12 in
(182.9 × 114.3 × 30.5 cm)

Uprooted Birdhouse
1987
Expanded polystyrene
polyurethane resin; latex
45 × 36 × 84 in
(114.3 × 91.44 × 213.36 cm)

Broken Bottle with Label Fragment
1987
Expanded polystyrene, canvas
polyurethane resin; latex
70 × 48 in diameter
(177.8 × 121.92 cm)

Razorblade, Nutshell, Bottle Cap
(Study of Small Objects in Light)
1956
Ink, pencil
11 × 8½ in (28 × 21.6 cm)
Musée nationale d'art moderne
Centre Georges Pompidou

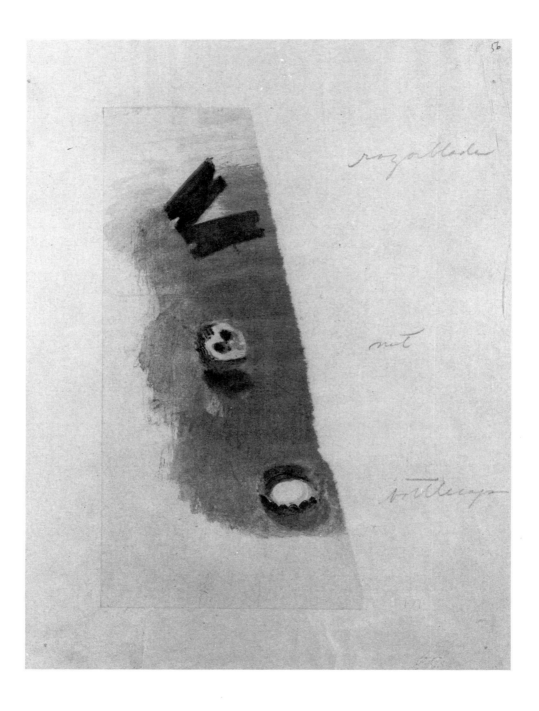

Injun
Dallas, April 1962
Performers in the barn

Injun
Dallas, April 1962
Performer on the barn

Injun
Dallas, April 1962
Reclining fiddle player
in the bedroom

The treatment of these vacant rooms may be compared with Oldenburg's use of a deserted farmhouse on the grounds of the former Dallas Museum of Contemporary Art for the staging of his performance *Injun*, in 1962. While walking through the empty rooms of the farmhouse, the artist was reminded of a scene in the film *The Man from Dakota*, which takes place at the time of the American Civil War. Playing soldiers, Wallace Beery and two others come upon a house in the woods, which they investigate room by room. Various objects in use, a cooking pot simmering on the stove, for example, indicate human presence but there is no one in sight. The incident ends with the discovery of the bodies of the recently murdered family in an upstairs room. In the farmhouse in Dallas, Oldenburg found himself identifying with the struggle for meaning and culture that had taken place in a deprived rural environment in the somewhat earlier period of the Depression and the Dustbowl. For *Injun*, the spectators reached the house in the dark, to be led repeatedly through the same rooms. Each room was inhabited by a different performer attempting in different ways to find some meaning in life. Through bizarre behaviour, costumes of secondhand clothes, and the use of battered objects bought in the local thrift shops, the performance evoked some of the bitter memories of tenant farmers forced into migration because of crop failures. These memories which floated in with the environment became an undercurrent of the performance. Through his imposition of a state of abandonment on Haus Esters, presently kept in such good repair, Oldenburg again points to the inevitable rise and decline of properties, families and cultures.

In the fall of 1956, when he had just arrived in New York, he would project his feelings of loneliness by drawing discarded, isolated objects. With the autumn light producing lengthy shadows, he would sit in his room and concentrate on a bottle cap, a bottle of lithographic ink, a razor blade. Chance groupings of objects in relationships that seemed dramatic to him would inspire poems in which the artist tried to enter the inanimate world:

rag asleep
furred with old questions
long trip in a wet thimble
a year among the pills

in brown melody
in a corked world
there can a good rag sleep
unafraid of time and arrogant pencils

In a play between calculation and the illusion of spontaneity, the objects in Haus Esters are placed so as to present a similar drama of still life. Things and emotions about things carry a powerful theatrical impact in Oldenburg's house, which he perceives as 'haunted' because 'art objects are living presences related to spooks.' Closest to a spook is the soft version of *Cross-section of a Toothbrush with Paste in a Cup on a Sink: Portrait of Coosje's Thinking*, his outdoor sculpture that was erected in front of Haus Esters in the autumn of 1983. Its muted colours relate it to the 'ghost' versions of household appliances that the artist began making in California in 1963, with *Light Switches*. Oldenburg would first make a model in cardboard or styrofoam, then reduce it to a pattern and have it sewn in canvas, as a sketch for the final soft sculpture in vinyl. The canvas 'ghost' versions, painted white, have a sheetlike gestalt, and appear 'spiritual' in comparison to the colourful vinyl pieces, matching Wallace Stevens's poetic thought: 'The

Dropped Muffler
1987
Canvas, aluminium, polyurethane foam
polyurethane resin; latex
36 × 40 × 108 in
(91.44 × 101.6 × 274.32 cm)

Cinderblock and Mortar Fragment
1987
Expanded polystyrene, steel
polyurethane resin; steel; latex
29½ × 36 × 32½ in
(74.3 × 91.4 × 82.6 cm)
Soft Folding Chair, Red
1987
Canvas, polyurethane foam; latex
62 in (157.5 cm, variable dimensions)
Mr and Mrs Ronald K. Greenberg
St Louis, Missouri

Half Tire with Deflated Tube
1987
Expanded polystyrene, plaster
polyurethane resin; latex
Tube: canvas, polyurethane resin; latex
Tire: 36 × 16 × 71 in
(91.44 × 40.64 × 180.34 cm)
Tube: 38 × 38 × 66 in
(96.52 × 96.52 × 167.64 cm)
Galerie Schmela, Düsseldorf

View of *The Street* as installed in the Judson
Gallery, New York, during the *Ray Gun
Show*, January 1960
A cripple (the balloon recalls those used in
comic strips); a screaming woman; a car
and a man on a bicycle (both bent into
the corner).

The Street installation
Street figures, a car

The Street installation
An airplane (upper left); a figure with a gun;
a dog and a running girl (both free-standing);
a van; the letters RAY (GUN is written on the
wall behind the head of the running girl);
the head of a mother; a child with a gun.

houses are haunted by white nightgowns.'[4] Oldenburg's original intention for Haus Esters was to select objects that might have been in use when the villa was still a home, and to complement them with the kind of things found in a sedate museum environment. The museum part, he thought, might be represented by a pedestal with a hoof broken off from an equestrian statue. The things thrown through the windows he associated with the rougher examples of contemporary art. For this group he first considered pairs of objects, one natural and the other shaped by man: a round rock together with a square brick, a branch with a cane, a charred log with a birdhouse. Then he pondered a mixture of single objects, such as a banana peel, an apple core, a leaf, a bone, a rabbit, a muffler, a chair, a galosh, a bottle, a pencil stub, a match. Eventually the categories coalesced into a group of ambiguous, highly suggestive broken objects extracted from the junk of the surrounding environment, discarded detritus combining nature and urban nature, all suitable for transformation and scaling up into sculpture through the chosen techniques of stiffened cloth or coated styrofoam.

A piece of wall made of cinder block, a construction material with no pretensions, is very different from the brick that Mies van der Rohe so cleverly applied in the construction of Haus Esters. Oldenburg also uses a fragment of brick, but the one in his selection is rendered worthless, being broken. The tree branch has become absorbed into the form of the muffler, which, in dropping off a car, has pulled part of the exhaust pipe with it. Furthermore, the outdoor sculpture *Cross-section of a Toothbrush*, despite its elite status as an artwork, has undergone the same fate as the other commonplace objects; like the birdhouse it has been uprooted and thrown, foundation and all, through the window.

Inside, however, it has lost its constructivist strength, turned soft. Its twisted parts remind one of a shed snakeskin, caught like a banana peel in the angle of a smashed windowpane. The bottle, set on its head so that its jagged edges face up, becomes an echo of a pedestal; the missing part of its torn label may hold the title of the sculpture. Finally, the idea of a twisted galosh has been replaced by that of the simplified but suggestive heel of a shoe, worn down on one side, with five nails sticking out of it. More than any of the other objects, *Lost Heel* recalls *The Street*, the installation Oldenburg did in January of 1960 in a small room of the Judson Gallery, New York, in which the city's tough street life was transformed into a metamorphic landscape like a war zone out of Céline.

While smaller figures on the walls indicated events at a distance, free-standing figures and objects, their flatness emphasized by black outlines, rose out of a rubble of old shoes, mattress springs, crushed pieces of metal, and so on. To capture their textural flavour, Oldenburg recycled materials he had found on the street: burlap bags, wooden crates, corrugated cardboard. The walls had the double identity of a picture plane and the surface of the street seen from a high vantage point. Painted white, like asphalt reflecting sunlight, they were filled with cut- or torn-out cardboard drawings of street events and figures. In *The Haunted House* the emphasis is less on the walls, which are left neutral, although their broken windows, which allow the outside to enter, are linked to the object fragments through the ambiguity of their two-dimensional picture planes turning into three-dimensional objects. With regard to the mise-en-scène of the object fragments Oldenburg

Crossection of a Toothbrush with Paste in a
Cup on a Sink: Portrait of Coosje's
Thinking, Soft and Uprooted Version,
with Foundation
1987
Canvas, polyurethane foam; latex.
Foundation: Expanded polystyrene;
Thoroseal, latex, 21 ft × 6¾ × 71⅝ in
(6.4 m × 17.19 × 181.9 cm)
Foundation 36 × 47 × 47 in
(91.44 × 119.38 × 119.38 cm)

Lost Heel
1987
Expanded polystyrene,
polyurethane resin; latex
49 × 44 × 12 in
(124.5 × 111.8 × 30.5 cm)

View through the window of *The Store*
107 East 2nd Street, New York
December 1961

recalls a time in the late 1950s in New York when several blocks were demolished on the Lower East Side:
'Between the place where I lived on 4th Street and Cooper Union, where I worked, I would pass by all these houses that had been ripped apart, so that you could see inside all the different rooms, and on the street you would find all kinds of relics and remnants of the home.'
These experiences became the basis for the performance *Blackouts*, 1960, a 'theatre of unrelated succession' in which the emphasis shifted from the activities of people in relation to things to things themselves. In one event from the performance, for example, Oldenburg, playing the 'Ragman,' moved in slow motion across the semi-dark stage with no other goal than to grab an illuminated rag on a ladder. The performer was just a tool to begin and end the plot; when he grabbed the rag, the lights went out — a 'blackout.' Likewise, *The Haunted House* evolves around the object fragments, the aftermath of human action, frozen in time. They are left behind; yet as the products of human thought they are indirectly connected with people, despite their collapsed state. *The Street* was derived from a violent, hopeless neighbourhood, New York's Bowery, where the distinction between squashed tin cans and bums lying around had been erased. *The Haunted House* is based upon the random objects of a vacant suburban lot, objects set in their casual positions by some disinterested force: a playing child, a passing vagrant, a gust of wind.

The debris that appears to have been thrown through the windows of Haus Esters, and to have landed in the rooms, lies randomly around, but Oldenburg has unified it through the use of styrofoam and cloth, materials very adaptable to transformation. He tends to choose subjects that echo his materials: the smooth white plaster in the pieces in *The Store*, for instance, from 1961–1962, represents such food as melting ice cream, while brittle styrofoam is used for crumbled building materials like the brickbat in *The Haunted House*. In the soft works, cloth is often used as a substitute for metal, as in *Soft Typewriter*, 1963, and in *Dropped Muffler*, where it is frozen into position with resin. In each object fragment Oldenburg takes care not to make the effect entirely sculptural, but to let the paint applied over the forms help to define them, as he did when he used 'paint coagulated into the form of an object' in the *Store* pieces.

In the object fragments Oldenburg applies colours individually, one over the other, on the highly textured, scraped, and abraded surface of the styrofoam, which has been hardened by layers of latex and resin. He compares it to a mountain landscape in which one layer of colour fills the valley, a second one covers the slopes, and a third the tops, so that they mix optically and take on a sculptural presence in their interplay between real and illusionary dimensions. Painting is conceived of as a material process. It is tricky to paint over rough surfaces. Oldenburg deals with the task by applying paint with a roller (which he prefers to a brush), by spraying or spattering it onto the surface, and also by pressing a paper towel soaked in it onto the surface. The paint can be thrown, dragged, or dabbed, but under no circumstances does the artist want to show his touch, unless he is simulating graffiti or a sign: *Cinder Block and Mortar*, for example, is a fragment of a red-painted wall with black graffiti on it. 'Beautiful' colour effects are avoided in favor of harsh harmonies; in the interest of verisimilitude some colours are deliberately jarring. The reinforcing rod sticking out of the wall fragment is of a brown colour that is disturbing in relation to the cinder block, to keep a 'unity of opposites' going.

Through texture and colour treatment, position and condition, Oldenburg freely links the otherwise different fragments, spooks, or stand-ins animating the haunted house of his own making. They are disparate as objects yet related in scale as sculptures. He creates a unity of associations, though the less evident and the more enigmatic they are the better. These object fragments are ghosts, in the sense that they evoke memories, which are different for each visitor. In Haus Esters the artist has left his belongings behind, broken archetypes. In the aftermath of action, rubble lies everywhere in the rooms of the broken-windowed main floor, like props on a stage after a performance, or like accidentally accumulated rubbish in *The Street*. But despite the wretched state of the debris, a remembrance of its splendid wholeness can still be sensed in the eroded geometry. We think we know whose stand-ins these are, for we can often identify a man by the contents of his pockets, or by a box filled with his possessions.[5] Yet the identification of the stuff with Oldenburg by congenial spirits arriving at the site is partly obscured, for the box containing the shards of these objects is signed by someone else: Mies van der Rohe.

Published in *Claes Oldenburg: The Haunted House*, Krefelder Kunstmuseen, 1987.

1. Unless otherwise noted, the quotations of Claes Oldenburg in this article come from discussions between him and the author.
2. Quoted in Claes Oldenburg, *Store Days* (New York/Villefranche-sur-mer: Something Else Press, Inc., 1967), p. 39.
3. Oldenburg uses 'Ray Gun' as an emblem applicable to every aspect of his work. In one disguise or another, 'Ray Gun' reappears, personified in this fragment of a prose poem, written in 1960–61, entitled 'Guises of Ray Gun'.
4. Wallace Stevens, 'Disillusionment of Ten O'Clock,' in *The Palm at the End of the Mind: Selected Poems and a Play* (New York: Vintage Books, 1972), p. 11.
5. The idea of a man being no more than the contents of his pockets, or than a box filled with his possessions, was strongly presented in *World's Fair II*, the final performance of Ray Gun Theater done in 1962 in *The Store*. The script reads, 'Lucas [Samaras] and John [Weber] enter carrying Dominic [Capobianco] in a suit stuffed with paper and debris as if dead. They place him on the table, slide him so he is in the middle, and go through his pockets, laying what they find on the tabletop around him. Turn him over etc. When his pockets are empty they push him to the edge of the table and carry him out.' The contents of his pockets included flags, jewellery, a flashlight, coloured paper, a wristwatch, and silverware.

Stranded Piano

Facing page:
*Project for Venice, Italy: A Fire Station
by Frank O. Gehry in the Form of a Snake
and an Office Building in the Form
of a Grand Piano Lid*
1984
Pencil, crayon and watercolour
$29^{15}/_{16} \times 34$ in (76×101.5 cm)
Collection Mr and Mrs Morton Mandel
Shaker Heights, Ohio

*Study for a Sculpture in the Form
of a Grand Piano*
1963
Cardboard, plaster, enamel
5⅜ × 11⅜ × 3½ in
(13.6 × 28.9 × 8.9 cm)
on base ¾ × 8 × 14 in
(1.9 × 20.3 × 35.6 cm)

The first attempt at a sculpture based on a grand piano was in Los Angeles in late 1963, part of the concern with furniture subjects which produced the *Bedroom Ensemble*, 1964. As with the furniture of the *Bedroom*, the piano was built on a rhomboidal plan, a literal rendition of representations of furniture in newspaper advertisements. The legs were eliminated, and the insides of the piano and the keyboard were filled with plaster to simplify the form. The result was something between a pie, a ship and an island (perhaps Alcatraz), which I painted all black.

Notebook Page: Grand Piano Shipwreck
August 1974
Pencil
One of a pair of drawings 2¾ × 5 in
(7 × 12.5 cm)
on sheet 11 × 8½ in (28 × 21.6 cm)

Ten or so years afterwards, the grand piano sculpture was taken up again, in two directions. In one, the piano was sited on a reef off-shore or on a beach, like a wrecked ship. The waves crashed over the sides, filling the body with water. This situation was probably inspired by reading that during the Great Fire of 1871 residents of Chicago took their pianos down to the shore of Lake Michigan and buried them in the sand.

A version intended for a beach in Cuba imagined that the piano had drifted over from Europe: the wreck of the Old World stranded on the shore of the New. The other direction focused on the lid itself, and culminated in a proposal for an office building in the form of a piano lid as part of a fantastic project for Venice, Italy, with Coosje and Frank O. Gehry in 1984.

Notebook Page: Hammock Study
1986
Clipping, pencil
11 × 8¼ in (28 × 21.6 cm)

Piano/Hammock
1987
Steel, painted; stainless steel; cast aluminium
16 ft l × 77 in × 63 in
(487.68 l × 193 × 160 cm)
Installed in the Konrad Fischer Gallery
Mutter-Ey-Strasse, Düsseldorf

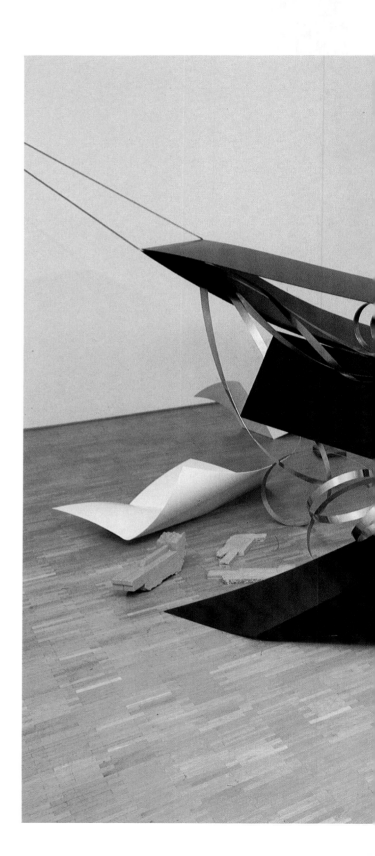

In 1983, we were asked to propose a
sculpture for the entrance space of the new
Fiorello H. La Guardia High School for
Music and Art in New York City. The grand
piano sculpture, combining music and art,
seemed an appropriate subject. Since the
floor was normally too crowded for a
sculpture, we suggested suspending a soft,
inverted version above the space. A model
was eventually developed in which the piano
was not soft but stretched out like a
hammock between two supports. The
proposal was not received very well, and we
withdrew, leaving the model to gather dust
for a couple of years. In the meantime, I had
built a model of the interior of Konrad
Fischer's one-room gallery on the Mutter-Ey-
Strasse in Düsseldorf, for a project involving
matches that had never been carried out. One
day I noticed that the piano/hammock
maquette would fit perfectly into the model
of the Fischer space, and so an alternate site
for the sculpture was discovered. The body,
made of stiff paper, like a cookie-cutter, was
drawn out to resemble a carriage spring,
which suggested the material of tempered
steel, such as that used for strapping bundles.
The theme of the piano/hammock is tension,
resistance to the force of gravity. Consistent
with the water situations of other versions,
the piano/hammock also looks like a
capsizing sailboat; the inverted lid, drooping
on the floor, is both a keel and a sail. The
insides of the piano spill out, the tensions of
the strings released, while the keys and music
pages scatter across the floor. One can
imagine the sound of a crash or a great
twang!

Notebook Page: Melody in Felt
1986
Felt pen
Sheet 5 × 2¾ in (12.7 × 7.1 cm) detail
from sheet 11 × 8½ in (28 × 21.6 cm)

In our home, the grand piano was played by
my mother, whose repertoire was limited to
the nineteenth century. People gathered
around it were likely to be European opera
singers visiting Chicago. I came to think of
the grand piano as a European subject, and in
my teenage years as a place of confrontation
between old and new: Liszt and Basie.

When asked to do an homage to Joseph
Beuys, a quintessential European, my first
thoughts were of the piano in his
work, especially the one muffled with felt,
which to me resembled an elephant.
Eventually, though, the piece took a different
direction, ending up as a 'Soft I' on a
cardboard pedestal.

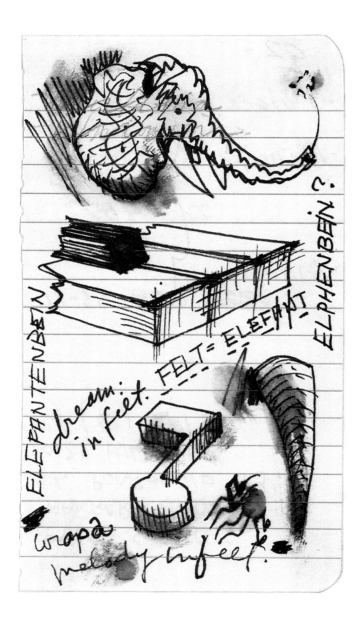

Colossal Monument Prepared with a
Mushroom and a Screw (for John Cage)
1987
Ball-point pen, felt pen
8¼ × 8¼ in (21 × 21 cm)
Collection Gilbert and Lila Silverman
Detroit, Michigan

Working on a contribution for an exhibition in homage to John Cage, I was playing around on the copying machine with a mushroom form torn out of the newspaper, when Coosje asked if I had ever read about the prepared piano. To my surprise I had not, and looked up 'How the Piano Came to Be Prepared' in *Empty Words*.

There I found the hard counterpart to the mushroom in the screw used by Cage to prepare the strings. A proposal followed naturally out of the ingredients. The wires hold the objects overhead; they bounce slightly, forming a passageway, as yet unlocated, perhaps in a shopping mall.

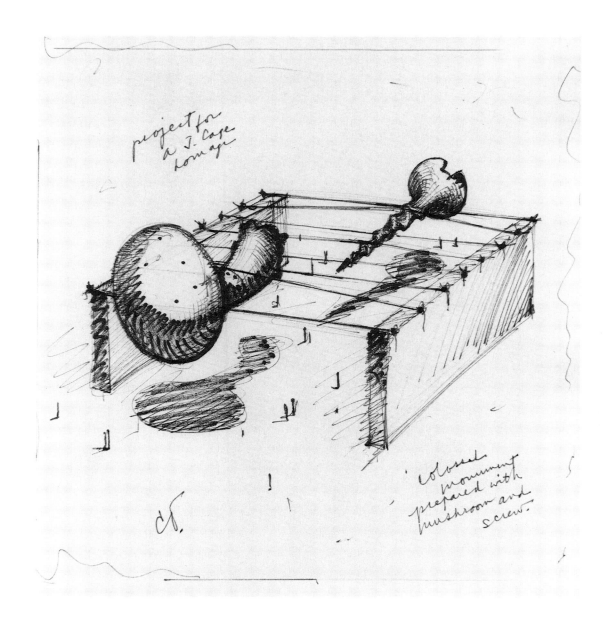

project for
a J. Cage
homage

'colossal
monument
prepared with
mushroom and
screw.

Bottle of Notes

Facing page:
*Notebook Page: Studies for
a Shipwreck Sculpture*
February 1987
Pencil, coloured pencil, felt pen
One of three sheets, assorted sizes
on sheet 11 × 8½ in (28 × 21.6 cm)

Notes Towards a Large-Scale Project
for Middlesbrough

Claes Oldenburg

The ingredient of the Middlesbrough site which most captured our imagination was the history of Captain Cook, whose birthplace and museum is advertised as an attraction of the area called 'Cook's Country' in the brochures. Captain Cook made us think of Captain Gulliver and his imaginary explorations earlier in the eighteenth century. For a while we tried out the idea of a sculpture based on the examination of Gulliver's pockets but to be called 'Cook's Pocket'. Coosje was later to read in Captain Cook's journals that the natives he encountered liked to pickpocket the explorers. But neither the objects obtained from Gulliver's pockets nor from the pockets of Cook's men (for example, a spyglass, a snuffbox) then seemed to us adaptable to a sculpture for the site, and only the idea of a container carried over to the next development. We had considered some kind of a vessel, for example, a shipwrecked sailing ship, but this subject required simplification and some connection to the idea of scale. We were reminded of Edgar Allan Poe's 'Ms. in a Bottle'. A bottle is a kind of ship, and ships are often built in a bottle. This provided the Swiftian reversal which authorized a very large bottle, or one as large as a civic sculpture needs to be, and so the bottle took the place of the sailboat.

One of the problems of the pocket subject had been its opacity, which could be solved by treating it as a cargo net, or, recalling Gulliver's net purse, in a way that the contents would be open to view. In a bottle the problem doesn't exist, but the net structure suggested a way to move from the object into the area of sculpture: instead of containing sheets of paper on which there was writing (another item from Gulliver's pocket), the bottle would be 'made of writing'. The paper would disappear, leaving only the script. The idea of a sculpture defined by lines occurs in the *Batcolumn*, in a more geometric way, as well as in the famous transporter crane over the Tees at Middlesbrough. We decided to use both our 'hands', which are quite different. I would do the drawing/writing surface of the *Bottle* in an angular style with ink blots, using some lines from Captain Cook's journals, in one colour. Inside would be a spiralling structure made of Coosje's rounded script in another colour, using a more personal text. We felt there should be a 'cork' in the *Bottle*; this would be the only solid part of the sculpture.

So far we have not brought the proposal into contact with the actual conditions of the site, but we visualize a scale of about 29 feet in height, which would make it almost 11 feet in diameter. The *Bottle of Notes* should be leaning at about the angle of the Tower of Pisa, as if stuck in sand by a receding wave. The surface could be a gravel plot within a park situation, preferably with a bit of a slope, perhaps near to some water.

Notebook Page: Cook's Hands, a Gate in
Middlesbrough, the Bottle on the Beach
1987
Three clippings, felt pen
on sheet 11 × 8½ in (28 × 21.6 cm)

gate

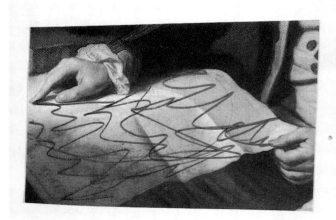

Notebook Page: Studies for a
Shipwreck Sculpture
February 1987
Pencil, coloured pencil, felt pen
Two of three sheets, assorted sizes
on sheet 11 × 8½ in (28 × 21.6 cm)

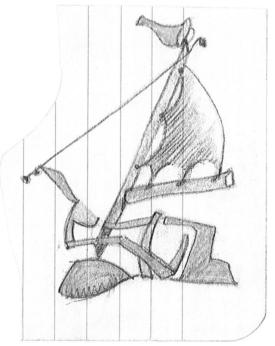

Shipwreck

Notebook Page: 'Britiship' and Bottle with Writing (detail)
1987
Pencil, felt pen
One of a pair of drawings 5 × 2¾ in
(12.7 × 7 cm)
on sheet 11 × 8½ in (28 × 21.6 cm)

Poster: 'New Media, New Forms I'
Martha Jackson Gallery
1960
Photoengraving
22⅝ × 17¾ in (57.5 × 45 cm)

When I first came to New York City in late 1956, what struck me most was the agitated writing on the surface of the city: the walls, the streets, every place that could be marked. Graffiti had not yet become self-conscious or stylized; these were anonymous messages of experience and survival.

I began to copy them and make monoprints which I put up in the city. After a while I made constructions out of the writing/drawing, using the patterns of newspapers and buildings. In a third stage, I began to see the spatial possibilities of the relation between writing and its ground.

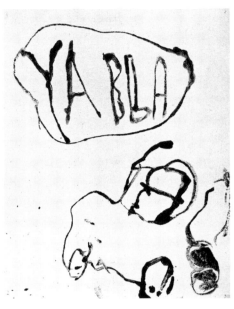

YA BLA and Man in Car
1960
Monoprint
24 × 18 in (61 × 45.7 cm)

Ray Gun Poster
1961
Sprayed oil wash on torn paper
24 × 18 in (61 × 45.7 cm)

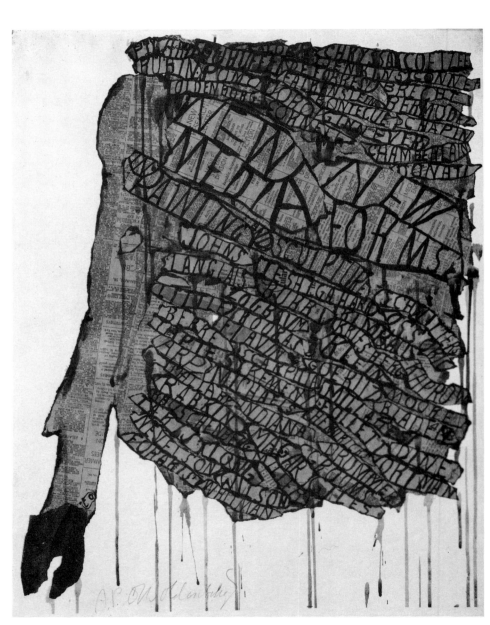

Study for the Spiral of Coosje's Script
in the 'Bottle of Notes'
1987
Pencil
11 × 8½ in (28 × 21.6 cm)
on a sheet 30 × 40 in
(76.2 × 101.6 cm)
together with other drawings

Bottle of Notes, First Study
1987
Felt pen on plastic bottle in cardboard
box filled with Pelliculite
9 × 3½ in diameter (22.9 × 8.9 cm)
in box 12 × 10 in (30.5 × 25.4 cm) and
*Cheese Dispenser in the Form
of the Leaning Tower of Pisa*
acquired c1979
Porcelain
8¼ × 2¾ in diameter (21 × 7 cm)

The first model was made by grabbing an
empty plastic Evian bottle, tearing off the
label and scribbling over the surface with a
felt pen. I cut the bottle, telescoped it to a
desired proportion, and stuck it in a box of
Pelliculite. It turned out that a certain scale of
writing had to be maintained for the visual
effect of the sculpture, so as not to reduce it to
a kind of filigree. For the outside we selected

part of a sentence from Captain Cook's
journals dealing with heaven and sea: 'we
had every advantage we could desire in
Observing the whole of the passage of the
Planet Venus over the Sun's disk'. For the
inside, we selected part of a text by Coosje
about the land near the sea, particularly the
North Sea: 'I like to remember sea-gulls in
full flight gliding over the ring of canals'.

Facing page:
Study for The Bottle of Notes
1987
Pencil, coloured pencil
30 × 25½ in (76.2 × 65 cm)

Biographies

Claes Oldenburg

Claes Oldenburg was born in Stockholm, Sweden, on 28 January 1929, but has resided in the United States almost continuously since 1930, first in New York City and Rye, New York, then from 1936 to 1946 and from 1950 to 1956 in Chicago, and again in New York from 1956 to 1976 and from 1978 to the present. He studied at Yale University (1946–50) and the Art Institute of Chicago (1950–54). Since 1976 he has been working on his 'large-scale projects' in partnership with Coosje van Bruggen. They were married in 1977.

Coosje van Bruggen

Coosje van Bruggen was born in Groningen, The Netherlands, on 6 June 1942. After receiving her Doctorandus degree in art history at the University of Groningen she became a member of the staff of the Stedelijk Museum in Amsterdam (1967–70), where she first met Claes Oldenburg. She co-edited the catalogue of the Sonsbeek '71 exhibition and taught at the Academy of Fine Arts in Enschede, from 1971 to 1976, and also did voice and translation for *Nothing to lose*, a record by Lawrence Weiner for the Van Abbe Museum in Eindhoven in 1976. She was a member of the selection committee for Documenta 7 in Kassel, 1982. Coosje van Bruggen is also author and director of the film *School Bus Yellow, Adirondack Green*, an account of large-scale projects and the *Flashlight* (Store Days Productions, co-directed by Machteld Schrameijer, 1981). She co-curated, with Dieter Koepplin, the exhibition *Bruce Nauman. Drawings 1965–1986* for the Museum für Gegenwartskunst, Basel, 17 May–13 July 1986, an exhibition travelling through July 1988. Besides books and articles on Oldenburg's work listed in the bibliography, Coosje van Bruggen is the author of *Maria Van Elk: tekenen 1973–1980*, Amsterdam, 1980; *Bruce Nauman*, New York, Rizzoli International, 1988; 'Richard Artschwager', *Artforum*, XXII, No. 1, September 1983, pp. 44–52; 'Gerhard Richter: Painting as a moral act', *Artforum*, XXIII, No. 9, May 1985, pp. 82–92. Coosje van Bruggen is currently preparing a monograph on the work of Lawrence Weiner (Lapis Press).

A Chronology of Large-Scale Projects
by Claes Oldenburg and Coosje van Bruggen
1976–1988

1976 **November**	*Giant Trowel*, painted steel, 12 m high, reinstalled on the grounds of the Rijksmuseum Kröller-Müller, Otterlo, Netherlands.	

1977
April

Batcolumn,
painted steel, 33.5 m high,
installed in front of the Social Security
Administration Building, West Madison Street, Chicago.

July

Giant Pool Balls (three),
concrete, each 3.5 m diameter,
installed in Münster, West Germany.

November

Mouse Museum (revised) and *Ray Gun Wing*,
installed at Art of the 20th Century, Vienna.

1979
October

Crusoe Umbrella,
painted steel, 17.06 m long
and 10.06 m high,
installed in front of the
Civic Center of Des Moines, Iowa.

1981
March

Flashlight,
painted steel, 11.73 m high,
installed at the University of Nevada, Las Vegas.

June

Split Button,
painted aluminium, 4.87 m diameter,
installed at the University of Pennsylvania, Philadelphia.

1982
March

Hat in Three Stages of Landing,
three 'hats', painted aluminium and steel, each 5.48 m diameter,
3.12 m high supported at different heights over a distance of 48.76 m,
installed on the grounds of the
Community Center in Salinas, California.

April

Spitzhacke,
painted steel, 10.25 m high, 12.25 m long,
installed on the bank of the
Fulda River in Kassel, West Germany.

1983
April–May

Gartenschlauch,
painted steel, consisting of a tube 50 cm diameter, 125 m long,
attached to a 'faucet' 11 m high
installed in Stuhlinger Park, Freiburg-im-Breisgau, West Germany.

June

The *Screwarch* project in the
Museum Boymans-van Beuningen, Rotterdam,
consisting of the *Screwarch*, painted aluminium,
3.80 m high, 2.44 m wide, 6.88 m long;
three large etchings and a model in painted bronze and aluminium
of the *Screwarch* bridge proposed for the Nieuwe Maas, Rotterdam.

November

*Cross-section of a Toothbrush with Paste, in a
Cup, on a Sink: Portrait of Coosje's Thinking*,
painted steel, 6 m high,
installed in front of the Haus Esters, Krefeld, West Germany.

**1984
April**

Stake Hitch,
painted aluminium and plastic materials consisting of a 'stake'
7.62 m, and a 'rope' and 'knot', approximately 12.19 m long,
installed in the Dallas Museum of Art,
Dallas, Texas.

May

Balancing Tools,
painted steel, consisting of three 'tools': 'hammer' 7.9 m,
'screwdriver' 6.7 m, and 'pliers' 7.76 m,
installed in front of the VITRA Factory,
Weil-am-Rhein, West Germany.

**1985
May**

Tube Supported by its Contents,
painted bronze and steel, 4.57 m high,
installed in Lohausen Park, near Düsseldorf, West Germany.

September

Coltello/Ship,
wood, steel and plastic, 25 m long (with blades horizontally
extended), a ship in the form of a Swiss army knife,
in the performance *Il Corso del Coltello*, Venice, Italy.

**1986
September**

Toppling Ladder with Spilling Paint,
painted steel and aluminium, 4.32 m high,
on the campus of the Loyola Law School,
Los Angeles, California.

Work in Progress

Free Stamp,
painted steel and aluminium,
14.63 m high on a base 9.45 m × 8.53 m,
for Cleveland, Ohio.

Dropped Bowl, with Scattered Slices and Peels,
painted concrete, steel and other materials,
a fountain in fifteen parts, covering an area of about 27.4 m square,
for the Downtown Government Center in Miami, Florida.

Spoonbridge and Cherry,
stainless steel and painted metal,
a fountain, 16.76 m long and 7.62 m high,
for the Walker Art Center, Minneapolis, Minnesota.

Selected Bibliography

Publications concerning Claes Oldenburg:

Claes Oldenburg
Store Days
New York, Villefranche-sur-mer, Frankfurt
am Main: Something Else Press, Inc, 1967
Documents from *The Store*, 1961, and *Ray
Gun Theatre*, 1962, selected by Claes
Oldenburg and Emmett Williams,
photographs by Robert R. McElroy

Gene Baro
Claes Oldenburg: Drawings and Prints
Lausanne: Publications I.R.L. (A Paul
Bianchini Book), London: Chelsea House
Publishers, 1969

Claes Oldenburg
*Proposals for Monuments and Buildings
1965–69*
Chicago: Big Table Publishing Company,
1969
Interview with the artist by Paul Carroll

Claes Oldenburg
*Claes Oldenburg Constructions, models, and
drawings*
Chicago: Richard Feigen Gallery, 1969

Barbara Rose
Claes Oldenburg
New York: The Museum of Modern Art,
1970
An exhibition circulated under the auspices
of the International Council of The Museum
of Modern Art, with introduction by Alicia
Legg and texts by the artist: Stedelijk
Museum, Amsterdam (foreword by Edy de
Wilde), Städtische Kunsthalle, Düsseldorf
(foreword by Karl Ruhrberg), The Tate
Gallery, London

Claes Oldenburg
Notes in Hand
Petersburg Press, 1971

Barbara Haskell
Claes Oldenburg: Object into Monument
Pasadena Art Museum, 1971,
with texts by the artist

Ellen H. Johnson
Claes Oldenburg
New York: Penguin Books (New Art 4),
1971

Claes Oldenburg
*Claes Oldenburg: Raw Notes; Documents
and scripts of the performances: Stars,
Moveyhouse, Massage, The Typewriter,*
edited by Kasper Koenig,
Halifax, Nova Scotia: The Press of the Nova
Scotia College of Art and Design, 1973

Susan P. Casteras
The Lipstick Comes Back
New Haven: The Yale University Art
Gallery, 1974

Götz Adriani, Dieter Koepplin and Barbara
Rose
Zeichnungen von Claes Oldenburg
Basel Kunstmuseum and Tübingen
Kunsthalle, 1975 (touring exhibition)

Martin Friedman
Oldenburg: Six Themes
Minneapolis, Minnesota: Walker Art
Center, 1975
Interview with Claes Oldenburg

Claes Oldenburg
Photo Log May 1974–August 1976
Stuttgart, London, Reykjavik: Edition
Hansjörg Mayer and New York: Store Days
Inc, 1976
and
Press Log May 1974–August 1976
Stuttgart: Editions Hansjörg Mayer and New
York: Store Days Inc, 1976

Robert Doty
Oldenburg: The Inverted Q
Akron, Ohio: The Akron Art Institute, 1977
Text by Claes Oldenburg

Coosje van Bruggen, Ad Petersen
*Claes Oldenburg: Tekeningen, aquarellen
en grafiek*
Amsterdam: Stedelijk Museum, 1977
(foreword by Edy de Wilde), exhibition
circulated to Musée National d'Art
Moderne, Centre Georges Pompidou, Paris
(foreword by Pontus Hulten) and Moderna
Museet, Stockholm (foreword by
Björn Springfeldt)

Coosje van Bruggen
*Claes Oldenburg: Mouse Museum / Ray Gun
Wing*
Cologne: Museum Ludwig, 1979

Claes Oldenburg and Coosje van Bruggen
*Claes Oldenburg: Large-Scale Projects,
1977–1980. A chronicle by Coosje van
Bruggen & Claes Oldenburg, based on notes,
statements, contracts, correspondence, and
other documents related to the works,*
essay by R. H. Fuchs
New York: Rizzoli International
Publications, Inc, 1980

Cor Blok
*Claes Oldenburg: Het Schroefboof-projekt;
een opdracht van Museum Boymans-van
Beuningen, Rotterdam 1978–1982. The
Screwarch Project commissioned by
Museum Boymans-van Beuningen,
Rotterdam 1978–1982*
Rotterdam: Museum Boymans-van
Beuningen, 1983

Claes Oldenburg and Gerhard Storck
*Claes Oldenburg: Cross Section of a
Toothbrush with Paste in a Cup on a Sink:
Portrait of Coosje's Thinking*
Krefeld: Krefelder Kunstmuseen, 1985

Claes Oldenburg, Coosje van Bruggen,
Frank O. Gehry and Germano Celant
El Cuchillo Barco, de Il Corso del Coltello
Milan: Electa and Madrid: Ministerio de
Cultura, 1986

Germano Celant, Coosje van Bruggen and
Claes Oldenburg
*The Course of the Knife/Il Corso del
Coltello, Milan: Electa, 1986*

*Gerhard Storck and Coosje van Bruggen
The Haunted House*
Krefeld: Krefelder Kunstmuseen, 1987

General publications, including reference to
Claes Oldenburg

Maurice Tuchman and Jane Livingston
*A Report on the Art and Technology
Program of the Los Angeles County Museum
of Art 1967–1971*
Los Angeles, California: Los Angeles County
Museum of Art, 1971
pp. 14–17, 19, 21, 23, 29, 36, 44, 241, 269

Ellen H. Johnson
*Modern Art and the Object: A Century of
Changing Attitudes*
London: Thames and Hudson, 1976
pp. 11, 33, 34, 37, 40, 127, 129–30, 135–40,
145–60, 165, 167, 202–04

*Documenta 6: Band III Handzeichnungen,
Utopisches Design, Bücher*
Kassel, 1977
pp. 200–01. Claes Oldenburg's notebook
pages selected by Coosje van Bruggen

Klaus Buszmann
pp. 200–01
Skulptur Ausstellung in Münster
Münster, 1977
pp. 71–73, 278–84

*Urban Encounters: Art, Architecture,
Audience*
University of Pennsylvania: Institute of
Contemporary Art, 1980
pp. 14–19, 34–35, 42, 52

Laszlo Glozer
Westkunst: Zeitgenössische Kunst seit 1939
Cologne: DuMont Buchverlag, 1981
pp. 236, 260, 263–67, 273–74, 276–77,
285, 450–57, 460, 502, 507–08

Rudi Fuchs, Coosje van Bruggen, Germano Celant, Johannes Gachnang, Gerhard Storck
Documenta 7
Kassel, Volume 2, 1982
pp. 246–69

Tony Knipe, ed.
Drawing in Air: An exhibition of sculptors' drawings 1882–1982
Sunderland: Sunderland Art Centre, 1983
pp. 130–32

A. A. Bronson, Peggy Gale and Jean-Cristophe Ammann
Museums by Artists
Toronto: Art Metropole, 1983
pp. 9–10, 259–70

Controversial Public Art From Rodin to di Suvero
Milwaukee, Wisconsin: Milwaukee Art Museum, 1983
pp. 9, 43–46

Ruth E. Fine, J. Carter Brown, Bruce Davis
Gemini G.E.L.: Art and Collaboration, A history of the unique relationship between artists and the Gemini workshop
Washington D.C.: National Gallery of Art and New York: Abbeville Press Publishers, 1984
pp. 11, 14, 19, 21, 25–27, 41, 62–71, 262

Barbara Haskell
BLAM! The Explosion of Pop, Minimalism and Performance 1958–1964
New York: Whitney Museum of American Art, 1984

Peter Davies and Tony Knipe
A Sense of Place: Sculpture in Landscape
Sunderland: Sunderland Arts Centre, 1984
p. 11

Howard Singerman, Richard Koshalek, Sherri Geldin, Julia Brown Turrell
Individuals: A Selected History of Contemporary Art 1945–1986
with essays by Kate Linker, Donald Kuspit, Hal Foster, Ronald J. Onorato, Germano Celant, Achille Bonito Oliva, John C. Welchman, Thomas Lawson
New York: Abbeville Press Publishers, Inc., 1986
pp. 110–13, 115–17, 119, 223–25, 297, 299, 300, 318–19

The Architecture of Frank Gehry
Minneapolis, Minnesota: Walker Art Center and New York: Rizzoli International Publishers, Inc., 1986
with commentaries by Frank Gehry and essays by Rosemarie Haag Bletter, Coosje van Bruggen, Mildred Friedman, Joseph Giovannini, Thomas S. Hines, Pilar Viladas
pp. 19, 47, 80, 101, 112–43, 188–89

Dominique Bozo
La Collection du Musée National d'Art Moderne
Paris: Centre Georges Pompidou, 1986
pp. 24–26, 455–56

Armin Zweite
Beuys ze Ehren
Munich: Städtische Galerie im Lenbachhaus, 1986
pp. 422–42

Karl Ruhrberg
Kunst im 20. Jahrhundert: Das Museum Ludwig-Köln
Cologne: Museum Ludwig, 1986
pp. 35, 38, 46, 214–16, 259

Lawrence Alloway
Pop Art: USA–UK American and British artists of the '60s in the '80s
Toyama: Toyama Museum of Art, 1987
with essays by Marco Livingstone and Masataka Ogawa
pp. 17–18, 53, 56, 143, 145

Prepared Box for John Cage
Chicago: Carl Solway Gallery, 1987
A tribute to John Cage

Iwona Blazwick, Sheena Wagstaff and Umberto Eco
Comic Iconoclasm
London: The Institute of Contemporary Art, 1987
pp. 9–10, 36

David Bourdon
'Artists' Dialogue: A Conversation with Claes Oldenburg'
Architectural Digest
vol. 39, no. 6, June 1982,
pp. 164, 168, 170, 172

Muni de Smecchia
'Gli Artisti nel loro studio Claes Oldenburg'
Vogue Italia
Speciale no. 6, March 1984, pp. 616–21, 664

Elisabeth Lebovici
'Dossier Claes Oldenburg Le matériau en action'
Art Press
no. 116, July 1987, pp. 13–21

Periodicals

Roy Bongartz
'Oldenburg draws Seven New Wonders of the World'
Horizon
vol. XIV, no. 2, Spring 1972, pp. 70–81

John Loring
'Oldenburg on Multiples: Multiples as concept and technology in the work of Claes Oldenburg'
Arts Magazine
vol. 48, no. 8, May 1974, pp. 42–45

David Shapiro
'Sculpture as experience: the monument that suffered'
Art in America
May 1974, pp. 55–58

Jeff Kelley
'Claes Oldenburg's "Flashlight"'
Arts Magazine
vol. 55, no. 10, June 1981, pp. 100–02

Photocredits